SPIRITUAL DISCOVERY SERIES

Facing MIDLIFE Challenges

RAYMOND T. BROCK

Radiant Life
1445 Boonville Avenue
Springfield, MO 65802-1894
02-0115

STAFF

National Director: LeRoy R. Bartel
Editor in Chief: Gary Leggett
Series Editor: Clancy Hayes
Assistant Editors: Gerald Parks
Lori Van Veen
Editorial Assistant: Diane Lamb
Design: Steve Lopez
Don Burchfield

Photo Credits:
©1996 PhotoDisc, Inc.: Cover, 4; Rick Davis: 16, 25, 88; Skjold Photographs: 34, 52, 61; Gail Denham: 7, 70; Borland Photos: 79; Jim Whitaker: 43.

Springfield, Missouri 65802-1894

Library of Congress Catalog Card Number 96-75255
ISBN 0-88243-115-3
Printed in the United States of America

A Leader's Guide for individual or group study with this book is available from Gospel Publishing House (order number 02-0215)

Contents

WELCOME TO THE SPIRITUAL DISCOVERY SERIES

We are glad you have chosen to study with us. We believe the discoveries you make through the use of the *Spiritual Discovery Series* will positively impact your life.

The *Spiritual Discovery Series* will challenge the user to ask questions of the biblical text, discover principles from the text, and make personal application of those truths. The Bible is the text. This guide is a tool for study.

The *Spiritual Discovery Series* is designed for use in either individual or group settings. Individuals will be excited by the discoveries made possible through a structured inductive study. Sunday School classes and other groups will find the *Spiritual Discovery Series* a valuable tool for promoting enlightened discussions centered on biblical truth.

How To Use This Study Guide

1 **Pray before beginning each study session.** Ask the Holy Spirit to illuminate your mind.

---

2 **Choose a translation of the Bible which you trust and can understand.** It will be helpful to have more than one translation available to aid your understanding of the biblical text.

---

3 **The Bible is your primary text.** Avoid using commentaries or reference books until after completing your own study. Reference works are best used to confirm your findings. On occasion, the study guide will direct you to use reference material. This is done when special insights are necessary for proper interpretation.

---

4 **Read the assigned biblical text at least twice before answering any questions.** This will provide an overview and focus on God's Word.

---

5 **Concentrate on the biblical passage which you are studying.** It is tempting to jump from one passage of Scripture to another in an attempt to make spiritual connections.

---

6 **Seek tangible ways to apply the principles gleaned from each study.** Bible study should never result in "head knowledge" alone. Bible study should lead to action.

Study 1

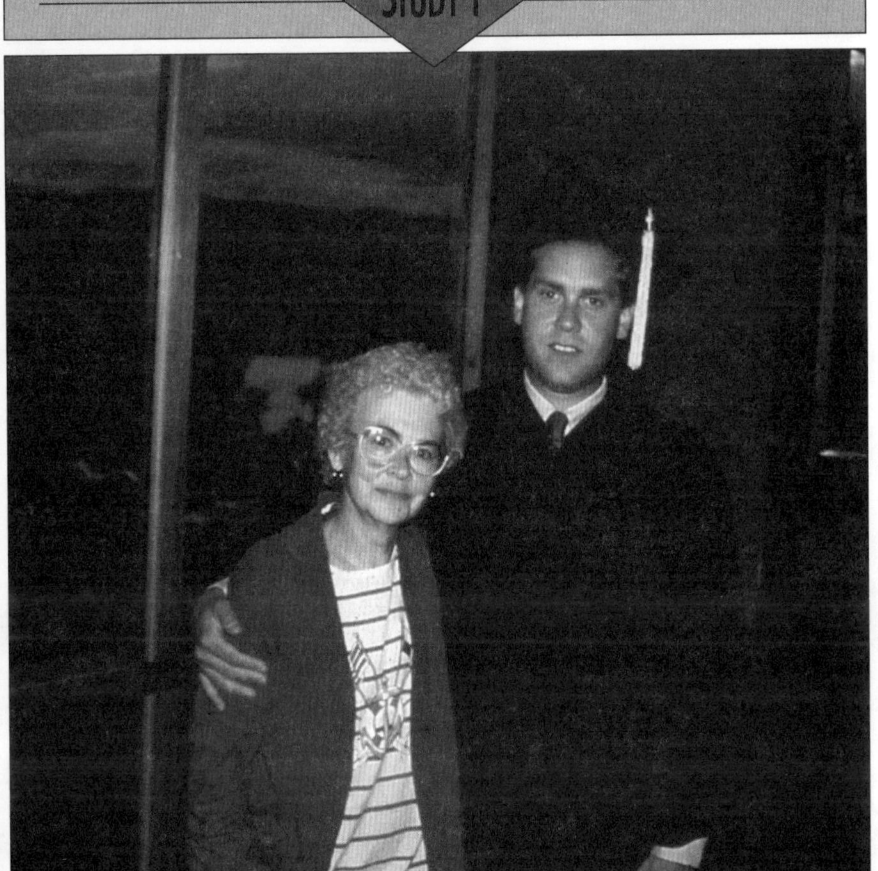

Transitions Of Life

The question, "When is an adult an adult?" used to have an obvious answer—18 or high school graduation. But things have changed. As a result of research by Gail Sheehy and other demographers, the passages of life have been revised to match current lifestyles. Conventional wisdom that had placed childhood from birth to age 12 and adolescence between 12 and 18 or high school graduation has been revised. Now childhood is said to be from birth to 10, plus or minus 2 years, with adolescence extending to 21, college graduation, or entering the workforce.

ADULT TRANSITIONS

Recent technology has extended adolescence to the late 20s and sandwiched in a short-term period known as *Provisional Adulthood. Provisional* adults enter the workforce early, marry young, and start their families. When does young adulthood begin? About age 30.

It has been noticed that children are entering adolescence younger than ever before. Both boys and girls are entering puberty (appearance of secondary sex characteristics) earlier than a century ago. It is not unusual for girls to show the first signs of puberty as young as 9 years of age with boys a couple of years behind.

Young people are staying in college longer, marrying later, and even living at home with their parents longer than any time in history. It is no longer uncommon for a young man still to be living at home with his mother in his middle 20s.

Provisional Adulthood (21 to 30)

Provisional adulthood is a period of disengagement, emotionally and geographically, from the family of origin. This is the age of decision when the baccalaureate and masters degrees are usually completed allowing for an entry-level employment position. Then the emerging adult is free to make the decision whether or not to get married. If the choice is marriage, this allows for the selection of a spouse. Those who do not complete these provisional adult tasks remain in an extended adolescence.

Failure to disengage from the family of origin in this period leads to *enmeshment*. This is a condition of extended familial attachment in which the "child-in-an-adult-body" is an appendage of the family rather than a maturing individual.

Young Adulthood (30 to 50)

The challenge of *young adulthood* is developing intimacy. If this is not achieved, the young adult drifts into isolation which will ultimately culminate in despair. Most of the vital decisions of life are completed during this time, including childbearing. Job and career choices started in the mid-20s deeply influence courtship and marriage decisions representing *young adulthood*.

Making enduring friendships and deciding whether to marry or not are the crucial choices at this point in life. Both single and married young adults must begin to develop intimacy—communication with other adults on a deep emotional level.

Intimate communication goes beyond surface talk about current and past events or about what other people are saying and doing. The conversation now shares what one thinks and believes. As the relationship develops, a person then shares on an emotional level his or her hopes and concerns for the future. Ultimately communication reveals the depths of one's cognitive and emotional life (Proverbs 8:6,7; Ephesians 4:25). In marriage this intimacy becomes the foundation for expressing meaningful sexual love.

Middle Adulthood (50 to 65)

Age 50 has been called the old age of youth and the youth of old age. The major task in this period is generativity, defined as a person who provides for others rather than for himself. If this task is not fulfilled the person will become self-absorbed—deepening the isolation begun in young adulthood—culminating in loneliness. Suicide rates for both never married and widowed men escalate during this period.

The onset of *middle adulthood* is marked by psychological and physiological processes which occur earlier in women than men. This phase of the adult passage will be discussed in detail in the remaining studies of this series.

Older Adulthood (65 to 85)

It is the last of the "Eight Ages of Man" theorized by Eric Erikson, the leading pioneer in studying the adult passages. He said the challenge of this period is to achieve integrity versus despair.

Successful transition in this passage comes from an appreciation of the continuity of the past, present, and future. The aging person accepts the life cycle and his or her own lifestyle. He or she is able to cope with the inevitabilities of life and can face death without fear or alarm.

Failure in *older adulthood* leads the person to believe that there is no meaning in human existence. He or she has lost faith in self and in others.

This person blames others for failure and wants a second chance at the life cycle with more advantages. There is no feeling of world order or of a spiritual sense in the universe. This person fears death and often experiences it as traumatic.

The anticipated life span is based on the assumption that illness and disease will not interrupt the living process. This life span grew from approximately 47 years at the beginning of the 20th century to 74 to 81 for men and 81 to 84 for women by the end of the century.

The satisfactions a person enjoys in this phase of life will be directly related to how retirement from the workforce is handled. Those who plan emotionally and financially for this transition find happiness as they disengage from the demands of a job or career. Ultimately retirement offers the freedom for planning one's own time and adventures.

✎ **1. Read Leviticus 27:1-7. In making vows to the Lord, what monetary value was placed on a person in late adolescence, young adulthood, and through middle adulthood?**

____

____

____

____

____

____

What monetary value was placed on those in older adulthood?

____

____

____

____

____

____

____

2. After reading Psalm 37:25 note David's perspective on life based on his life experience from youth to old age.

Extended Adulthood (85 to 100+)

Those who have lived past 85 years of age report it is a time of reflection, of looking back over a life that usually has been well-spent. Aging is an extremely complex phenomenon and the human life span is physically fixed. Currently the accepted maximum life potential for humans is set at about 114 years.

3. What did Solomon say about the marks of old age? (Proverbs 16:31).

PSYCHOSOCIAL CHALLENGES OF MIDLIFE

Success in navigating the midlife passage of adulthood requires continuing to be, or becoming, a productive and creative person. Work productiveness is not so much for one's own self as for the family. This involves taking pride in one's children and guiding them into becoming fully functioning adults. Also, adults in midlife must deepen the intimacy in their marriage to continue their relationship through the rest of the adult passage. Otherwise they may face marital problems.

A unique phenomenon emerged in the last half of the 20th century. Persons in midlife commonly assist their own parents in adjusting to the changes they are facing in their golden years. They discovered that their parents were living longer than their grandparents had lived, bringing additional responsibilities.

During middle adulthood, life is enriched by friends from the past as well as new friendships. This is the time to engage in the creative adventures of self-discovery. It is also the time when adult maturity is crystallized. They have reached the top of the mountain and the middle of the life span. Those who have studied the processes of aging have identified the following characteristics of mature middle age.

- They have developed a clear personal identity demonstrated by an intimate, loving relationship with a mature member of the complementary sex. Together they take on the responsibilities of rearing their children.

- They assume personal responsibility for their own behavior. They respond appropriately to the decisions of authorities who have been placed over them and to those who serve under them in the corporate structure.
- They pursue independently their own goals. Recognizing their own limitations, these persons seek advice from others when it is appropriate.
- They maintain and enjoy interpersonal relationships with others. As a result, they make allowances for their deficiencies with understanding and tolerance. They recognize that everyone is fallible and makes mistakes.
- They are attentive to their family and vocation. They also engage in constructive leisure-time activities without being demanding or selfish.
- They are generally free from the symptoms of physical or emotional illness and lead fully functioning lives as mature adults.

Failure to make the midlife transition leads to becoming egocentric. The person indulges in excessive self-love because of having drifted away from the support of family and friends. This leads to personal impoverishment and self-indulgence. Addictive behavior associated with the youth passage will resurface: i.e., cigarette smoking, alcohol consumption, drug use, obesity, poor diet, etc. Feelings of helplessness and hopelessness can lead to disillusionment.

The self-absorbed person can become a workaholic. While satisfying his selfish desires over the family's needs, the family becomes estranged. Work becomes a mistress even if sexual liaisons are not solicited. Not only does the person become nonproductive, but forced, early retirement can occur due to severe physical deterioration. This is a result of psychosomatic health problems rather than organic conditions or corporate downsizing.

Developmental Tasks Of Midlife

In order to avoid failure in the midlife passage, there are eight tasks the person should undertake.

Task number one: **Relate to one's spouse as a person.**

It is important to maintain an active, loving relationship with one's spouse through and beyond the childbearing years. Strain comes on the midlife marriage if one parent or the other has invested more into the children than into the marriage.

The axiom is true: There is life after children! In fact, some of the most exciting times in marriage can be enjoyed after the children have been launched into a life of their own. So, it is essential to keep the original romantic spark alive into and through this period of life to fully enjoy the "empty nest."

4. Read Ephesians 5:33. What attitude should a husband and wife have for each other as they move through midlife?

____

____

____

____

____

Task number two: **Establish and maintain an economic standard of living.**

A person should be in charge of his or her work rather than letting work determine one's life. Vocational excellence and financial freedom are the result of a creative attitude toward work and are an expression of one's identity.

If the size of the person's paycheck is the measure of self-esteem, failure may follow the retirement party. The relevant question is: "Who will you be when you are no longer defined by your work?"

Navigating this task can insure an adequate retirement income by establishing a savings plan and investment program.

5. Read Numbers 8:23-26. How did reaching the age of 50 affect the Levite males of the Old Testament vocationally?

---

6. What importance did Paul put on husbands and fathers providing adequately for their family during their working years? (1 Timothy 5:8).

Task number three: **Assist teenage children to become responsible adults.**

Parents have a biblical obligation to allow—even encourage—their children to leave the family of origin and cleave to the marital partner of their choice (Genesis 2:24).

Once a child has married, any emotional and financial assistance parents give the young couple should be only when requested and then given with no strings attached. Otherwise, "gifts" become disguised "bribes" which interfere with the establishing of a strong marital bond by the young couple.

7. Read Genesis 27:1-5,22-24,30-33. How did Isaac provide for his family in his old age?

---

8. In Proverbs 17:6, what did Solomon reveal about relationships from an older person's perspective?

____

____

____

____

Task number four: **Adjust to aging parents.**

This is a new phenomenon in the Western world because of the increasing life span. Parents are living longer than ever before. Even when aging parents are in good health and remain in their own homes they are a concern to their adult children.

Task number five: **Develop adult leisure-time activities.**

Older adults seldom engage in and enjoy leisure-time activities that they did not at least experiment with in their younger years. It is essential that middle-age adults be involved in activities they can enjoy when aging brings more time with less money and less energy.

Task number six: **Accept and adjust to physiological changes.**

Aging is an extremely complex phenomenon. There are many different types and rates of aging that occur, influenced by both genetic and environmental factors. Unfortunately, aging is irreversible and progresses whether we can see it or not.

Fixed aspects of aging include: arterial wall rigidity, cataract formation, graying of the hair, loss of kidney reserve, thinning of the hair, and loss of elasticity of the skin. A healthy diet and regular exercise are major requirements for the slowing down of the aging process in midlife. Each faculty of the body has a unique exercise regimen that can be learned and practiced.

Task number seven: **Achieve adult civic and social responsibility.**

The community needs the involvement of Christians in midlife. This is when leadership is needed to sustain community welfare. Good citizenship requires that Christians make responsible decisions at the polls and support candidates for office who will make decisions for the common good. Many civic and government leaders are chosen from among Christian men and women in the middle of their adult years.

9. What gifts does Job 12:12 list regarding old age that can contribute to community welfare?

____

____

____

____

____

10. Read Romans 15:1,2. What should be the attitude of the Christian in dealing with neighbors and friends? (See also Luke 10:27; Galatians 5:13,14.)

____

____

____

____

____

Task number eight: **Develop and maintain an intimate relationship with God.**

Individuals in their middle years need to maintain a practical devotional life that demonstrates real Christianity to the world. Involvement in church and community religious activities illustrate the relationship between Christ and the Church. Commitment to a body of believers is essential in meeting the needs of midlife.

11. How does Ephesians 5:25-32 indicate your marriage can be a Christian witness?

____

____

____

____

____

____

SUMMARY

Aging is inevitable as we march from the cradle to the grave. Wise is the person who anticipates the developmental tasks of each phase of life. The path of aging is not always smooth. Some of the changes are dramatic, some traumatic, and others slip by unnoticed. Those who prepare themselves mentally, emotionally, spiritually, and physically for the transitions can face aging with anticipation rather than despair.

In this study we have focused on the midlife period between age 50 and 65. By God's good graces we have the first half of life to prepare for this transition. One observer noted, "Until we are 35 or 40, our faces are those God gave us; after that they are the faces which we made for ourselves." Why not strive to make it a "smiley face"?

LET'S REVIEW

1. What are the four stages of adult life? Summarize each one.

2. List below the indications of traversing the midlife passage successfully.

3. What denotes failure in making the midlife passage?

4. Why is it of primary importance to strengthen one's marriage in midlife?

5. How can the marriage of the parents affect their children who are being launched into adulthood?

6. What steps should be taken in midlife to insure making a smooth transition into older adulthood?

STUDY 2

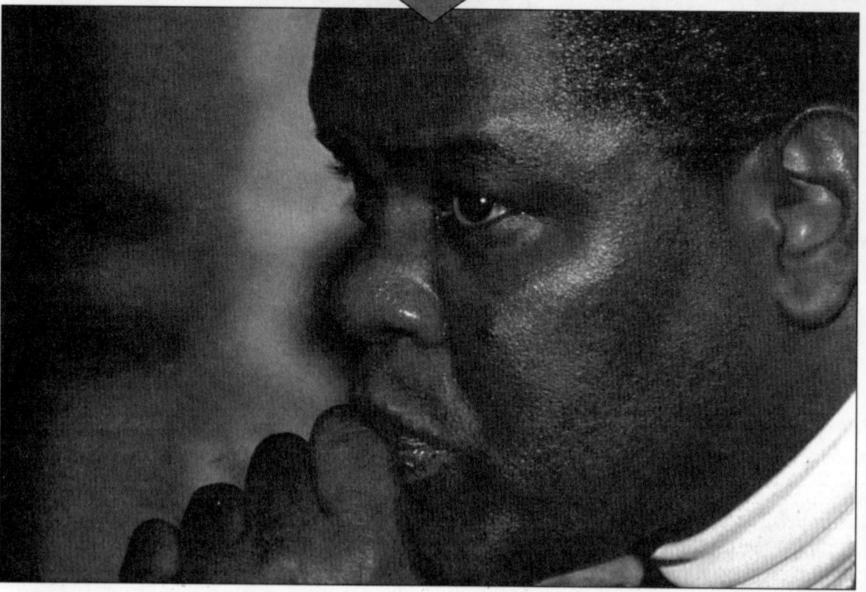

WHEN YOU DON'T FEEL FULFILLED

Many people spend their whole lives looking for fulfillment and never find it. Philip II left his son, Alexander, the small Greek principality of Macedonia. Starting with this, Alexander the Great's army conquered Greece, Turkey, Syria, Iraq, Iran, and northern India.

Historians report that standing on the top of the mountains separating India and China, Alexander wept convulsively. Why? His troops refused to follow him into China. They were tired of fighting and wanted to savor the fruits of their victories. He wept because there were no more worlds to conquer.

Alexander turned to wine, women, and song. He married Roxanne, the most beautiful princess of his conquered peoples, and died at age 33. In spite of being one of the most famous rulers of the ancient world and one of the greatest military strategists of history—he was still unfulfilled.

MIDLIFE DEFINED

Fulfillment

Fulfillment is "the state of being full, satisfied, satiated, or of being without lack." Look at a 1 cup measuring cup. When it is full it holds 1 cup. But when its contents only come to the halfway mark, is the cup half empty? Or is it half full?

This all depends on how you look at it. The optimistic person sees the cup as half full, but the pessimistic person sees it as half empty. Satisfaction in life is like that. It all depends on your point of view.

Our discontent in life is in direct proportion to how realistic our expectations are. When we set goals for ourselves based on the gifts and talents the Lord has given us, we thrill at our accomplishments. When our goals are unrealistic and we fall short of achieving them, we are disappointed.

The same thing applies in interpersonal relationships. If we have expectations for others they cannot—or choose not to—fulfill, we will be disappointed. Our disappointment will be in proportion to how unrealistic our expectations of them have been.

1. Read Psalm 37:4. What does David tell us to do in relationship to the Lord? What is the promised result?

____

____

____

____

____

2. What desire of David's will need to be ours if we are to find fulfillment in Jesus? (Psalm 40:8).

____

____

____

____

Contentment

Contentment is "the state of being contented, satisfied, and at peace with ourselves and our situation." When we sing, "There is no disappointment in Jesus," we are declaring that we are content in Him—He is all that we expect Him to be. Such contentment brings joy and peace. So we sing, "All is well with my soul."

On the other hand, contentment does not mean that all is well with the world. You can be contented in Christ and still aware of the lost world which needs to be introduced to Him. Contentment in Christ encourages a faithful witness for Him and strives to bring others into a personal relationship with Him.

3. What was Paul's attitude, recorded in Philippians 4:12, toward the high points and low points of his life?

4. Read 1 Timothy 6:6. What does Paul tell Timothy the source of great gain is in the Christian life?

Happiness

A lot of people desire happiness. They do not realize that happiness cannot be found in pursuing it. One scholar puts it, "Happiness cannot be pursued, it ensues." *Happiness* is like the "holy grail" of medieval mythology; just as you think you have found it and reach out for it, it eludes you. It is the elusive dream that slips between your fingers.

But when we obey God under the direction of the Holy Spirit, we will find true happiness. We are enveloped in the joy and peace that come from doing God's work in His way at His time. These are the sacred moments in life.

5. After reading Ecclesiastes 5:18-20, detail below the attitude Solomon says we should have toward our work.

6. Read 2 Timothy 1:11,12. On what does Paul base his contentment?

Complacency

May the Lord never let us become complacent! *Complacency* is "contentment with the status quo; self-satisfaction accompanied by unawareness of actual dangers or deficiencies." Complacency would blind us to the needs of the lost and lead us into lethargy. This is no time for the Christian to be passive about the claims of Christ on humankind. This is the time to be active in fulfilling the Great Commission (Matthew 28:19,20).

7. In the Luke 12:13-21 account of the rich man's efforts to bring fulfillment to all of his plans, what was his attitude toward the fruits of his labor?

____

____

____

What did God think of the rich man's attitude and plans for the future?

____

____

DEVELOPING A WORLD VIEW

Our thoughts greatly influence the way we view the world around us. Developing a world view requires us to develop a philosophy of life which guides our thoughts and actions. This philosophy of life is shaped by opinions, beliefs, attitudes, and values.

Opinions

Opinions are "simple thoughts." They are easily altered when circumstances change. One can say, "This is a beautiful day." Depending upon one's perspective a "beautiful day" can be sunny or rainy. Opinions are the least stable of any conclusion.

Beliefs

A *belief* is anything to which we add the prefix, "I believe." It may be a firmly held opinion, or it may be a doctrine of the church we accept. It is a belief because we say it is, not because there is something inherent in it that makes it true. Beliefs are more stable than opinions, but they can change under persuasion or conviction.

Attitudes

Attitudes are much more stable than either opinions or beliefs. They are extremely important to us and influence our behavior. Attitudes cannot be measured—they can only be inferred by behavioral demonstration. If we believe something, our actions will show it. Our actions evidence the attitude which motivates that behavior.

An attitude is a predisposition to respond to the opportunities of life—people, places, things, and ideas. Attitudes have a cognitive component (thinking), an affective component (feeling), and a behavioral component (action). They reflect our whole personality and become an expression of who we are.

8. **Read Philippians 2:5-8. Discuss the following question below. "Why is it important for Christians to develop the attitudes of Christ?"**

____

____

____

____

9. **After reading the Beatitudes in Matthew 5:1-12, list the attitudes that fulfill God's will for one's life.**

____

____

____

____

Values

Values are the most stable of our thoughts. They reflect what is dearest to us—what we are willing to live by and die for.

It has been estimated that a person has hundreds of thousands of opinions, thousands of beliefs, several hundred attitudes, but no more than one or two dozen values. Values are not altered by the winds of change. Values change only when the core of the personality is restructured such as in conversion to a philosophy of life or a religious belief.

When we value Jesus, every aspect of our lives should reflect the presence of the indwelling Christ. Then our opinions, beliefs, and attitudes will reflect our values.

DECISION MAKING AND PROBLEM SOLVING

To find fulfillment, it is important for us to learn the difference between *decision making* and *problem solving*.

Decision Making

A *decision* is selecting from among two or more alternatives of equal value. There is a 50 percent chance of being right and a 50 percent chance of being wrong when each option is potentially correct. Here are the steps in *decision making*:

1. Define the decision to be made.
2. Determine what is important and why.
3. Examine the information at hand.
4. Seek new information as needed.
5. Assess the risks involved in the decision.
6. Develop a plan of action.
7. Prayerfully make the decision.
8. Evaluate the effectiveness of the decision making process for future decisions.

10. Describe the situation that faced Moses which his father-in-law helped him resolve that is recorded in Exodus 18:17-24. Summarize Jethro's recommendation.

____

____

____

11. Review Joshua 24:15,16. What influence did Joshua's decision have on his family—and the whole nation of Israel?

____

____

____

12. According to Psalm 1:1-3, what are the rewards for the person who uses Scripture as a guide in decision making?

____

____

Problem Solving

Problem solving seeks to find the best solution among unequal options. As a result, there is one best decision frequently discovered through trial and error. Here is the process of *problem solving*:

1. Activate solvable problems.
2. State and limit the problem.
3. Find needed information.
4. Process the information.
5. State and test possible solutions.
6. Find the most workable solution.
7. Evaluate the effectiveness of the problem solving process for future use.

13. Read Proverbs 15:22. Why is it important to seek godly counsel when we are faced with decisions and problems in life?

____

____

14. How does studying and memorizing the Word of God help us in decision making and problem solving? (Psalm 119:105).

____

____

15. According to John 14:26, why was the Holy Spirit sent to believers? How can He help us in decision making and problem solving?

____

____

____

SPIRITUAL COMMITMENT

In order to be truly fulfilled in life, we must examine our relationships. Mark 12:28-31 puts these relationships into perspective.

Relationship With God

Our relationship with God is the most important relationship of our lives. We are to love God with all our heart, soul, mind, and strength. This is the sum total of the human personality.

Mark 12:28-31 is the most complete description of personality in all literature. It includes our cognitive life (heart and mind), our affective life (emotions or feelings), and our behavior (strength). We choose to love God with all of our capacity as human beings created in the image of God.

16. What important decision must each individual make? (Matthew 6:24).

____

Why is it essential that this decision be made?______________________

____

17. Read Matthew 6:25-34. What is the logic of putting God's will first in our lives?

____

____

Relationship With Ourselves

We are to love our neighbor as we love ourselves. If we do not love ourselves, we will not be able to love others as we should. A healthy self-concept sees ourselves as children of God and joint-heirs with Jesus Christ receiving all of the blessings God has for us.

This is not a narcissistic self-love or love of self. It is accepting ourselves as God has made us.

18. Read Romans 12:3. What is the proper way to view oneself?

____

____

19. In Philippians 4:4-7, what does Paul say our attitude should be when we are tempted to be overly concerned about conditions around us?

Relationship With Others

Love of others radiates out from us in concentric circles. Our most important neighbor is our spouse. Our children and our extended family are our next circle. The circles spread from there to include the body of Christians who worship with us and our colleagues at work. They extend further, taking us into all the world while we carry the gospel to every creature as the Great Commission commands.

20. Based on Matthew 5:16, how should Christians relate to the world around them?

---

21. Read Matthew 5:43-45. What new concept is introduced into human relationships by the coming of Christ into the world?

---

22. What new commandment, beyond those in the original Decalogue, does Jesus give in John 13:34,35? How could this command revolutionize your world?

SUMMARY

This study highlighted some of the strategies we can use when we do not feel fulfilled in life. Some people seem to be plagued with a basic discontent. Others find ways of seeing the "silver lining in the dark cloud" and a "rainbow after the rain."

We have looked at fulfillment, contentment, and happiness as positive states of mind and distinguished these from complacency, which is passive rather than active.

We also looked at the different approaches to developing a world view and noted the importance of adopting a set of workable values in life. Then we distinguished between decision making and problem solving.

Finally, we examined the importance of our spiritual commitment to love God and others to the degree that we love ourselves. We can do this only as we receive God's love which is fully poured out upon us as we seek to follow Him.

LET'S REVIEW

1. What attitudes should we develop if we feel unfulfilled in life?

2. In what way are attitudes and values more important than opinions and beliefs in developing a world view?

3. What is the basic difference between a decision and a problem?

4. Why should a person's relationship with God be the highest value in the life of a Christian?

5. How does our attitude toward ourselves influence our relationships with others?

Study 3

Reevaluation Of Life Goals

Have you ever started on a trip and had no idea where you were going? If so, you never knew when you arrived. "How foolish!" you say. Yet many people launch activities in life with no idea where they are headed.

Why did you get married? Why didn't you get married? If you did marry, why did you marry the person you did at the time you did?

Having goals is essential in all facets of life. If we do not have goals, we lack purpose. Lack of purpose keeps us from realizing our God-given potential.

In this study we will discover how to set goals and to periodically reevaluate them. A goal made at the beginning of a relationship may need to be altered later because of the transitions that come with aging. Knowing when and how to revise goals in family relationships is extremely important.

SETTING GOALS

The three dimensions of goal setting are: *short-term*, *long-term*, and *intermediate*.

1. Read Matthew 7:24-27. What observations did Jesus make regarding the setting of goals that would endure forever?

Short-term Goals

Immediate goals are *short-term* and deal with the present. They may be made by the day or by the week.

At the beginning of a day, ask yourself, "What do I wish to accomplish today?" Make a list. This should include all of the major tasks you wish to accomplish in that one day. Check off each activity as you complete it. At the end of the day look at what you have accomplished. If the list has not been completed, ask yourself why.

Maybe you tried to accomplish more in the day than was humanly possible. Maybe you did not allow sufficient time for each task. It could be you allowed yourself to become distracted and did some other things that were not on your list. Evaluate what went wrong.

It is better to have a short list and be able to complete it than to have a long list filled with uncompleted tasks. Move the uncompleted tasks from today and use them to start the list for tomorrow. Shorten the list so you can finish all the tasks you have set for yourself.

If you do this consistently you will be surprised how much you can accomplish in a day. And you will be surprised at how good you feel when you complete all the tasks on your list for several days in a row.

Some have found it is more effective to make goals by the week. This allows more flexibility and breaks up the monotony of daily list-keeping. Planning a week at a time also permits scheduling larger blocks of time to fulfill projects. The result is more efficient use of time and energy. It also emphasizes the difference between the urgent and the important.

Christians must focus on doing what is important instead of being distracted by the urgent. Paying attention to urgent tasks is more like putting out fires than planning creatively for the future.

Long-term Goals

Long-term goals lead to the completion of a significant task and may take years to accomplish. When people enter college, they often have a major course of study in mind and know which degree they want to earn. After graduation, they then project another goal that reflects what they want to accomplish in graduate school or in the world of work. Such goals are essential to accomplishing significant goals in life.

2. What *long-term* goals does God have for His children based on Jeremiah 29:11-14?

 **3. Read Colossians 3:1-4. Our goals should be based on what system of values?**

Intermediate Goals

Intermediate goals lie between *short-term* and *long-term* goals and take months to years to complete. They are the bridge that connects the present with the future. For those who attend college, getting from their freshman year to their senior year requires a series of *intermediate* goals as they choose each course and complete each assignment. Looking back on it after graduation, it appears like one smooth transition. The same process works at each stage of the adult passage if we learn to utilize this strategy effectively.

It is essential that we remain flexible when making plans. Sometimes circumstances force us to change from our original plans and take a different direction altogether.

4. After reading 2 Corinthians 1:12 through 2:2 note below how Paul's plan to visit the Corinthians changed. Why did he not come to them as originally planned?

REEVALUATING GOALS

There are facets of our adult lives that require us to reevaluate our goals periodically.

5. What does Paul say our attitude in life should be? (Colossians 3:17).

Relationships

Family relationships need to be reevaluated as changes come in the family. A child is born. The child enters kindergarten and, before you know it, graduates from high school. An adult child leaves home. A family member dies. A job is lost. All of these are crisis points that require the reassessment and revision of goals. Sometimes the new goal requires making a significant change. Other times the decision will be to maintain the status quo. But these transition events should not pass without evaluation and making the appropriate adjustments in lifestyle.

6. Read 1 Chronicles 28:4-7 and detail below how David decided which of his sons should succeed him as King of Israel.

How can David's example help give confidence when setting goals in your life?

____

____

Husband and wife relationships need to be reviewed frequently. It is important to keep romance alive in the marriage and to continue dating after the courtship phase is over. Couples who plan times to be together, who maintain a loving relationship, and who engage in open communication are much happier in their older years than those who let their relationship die.

7. What should be the attitude of a husband and wife toward each other as outlined in Ephesians 5:21 through 6:4?

____

____

What should be the relationship of children to their parents?

____

____

Occupation

At the end of the 20th century there was an upheaval in the job markets around the world. Stable businesses and factories were folding or being absorbed in takeovers that were sometimes hostile.

At the beginning of the 20th century a person could expect to work for the same employer for an entire working career because of the stability of the job market. By the middle of the century changes in the workplace indicated that flexibility was more important than training for a specific job. By the end of the century an adult could expect to make as many as five or six significant job changes during the working years.

8. Read Matthew 4:19,20. How did the call of Jesus change the career of Peter and Andrew?

____

____

What adjustments do you think this forced them to make?________________

____

____

As the years passed, it also became evident that those in management must select their successors early. Those currently in management must prepare their successors to assume the responsibilities of corporate leadership and help them develop in a leadership role.

9. Read Exodus 33:11. At what point in his career as leader of the Children of Israel did Moses select Joshua to succeed him?

____

____

How long was Joshua in training?

____

____

10. What does the writer of Ecclesiastes say in Ecclesiastes 9:10 about a person's attitude toward work?

____

____

How would this attitude help relieve boredom in the workplace? ____________

____

What does this suggest to those who cannot or do not work in such a fashion?

____

____

Social

Social changes are often influenced by an unstable job market. Transfers and firings keep people on the move. It is not unusual for a family to move every 3 years because of job transfers and plant closings. As society becomes more mobile, friendships become unstable unless tremendous effort is made to keep in touch by long-distance. How to make friends and work through the grief of moving and losing friends become major challenges for family members of all ages.

11. In Proverbs 18:24, what does Solomon say about being wise in choosing friends?

____

____

____

12. Read James 2:23. On what basis was Abraham called a friend of God?

____

____

How does friendship with God help if one is faced with social upheaval? ______

______

Leisure

With the cutting back of the work week and changing to 4-day working schedules, a new look has come to leisure time activities. More time is available for athletic events as well as such aesthetic activities as art, music, and literature.

How to utilize this time without splitting up the family becomes a major challenge. The temptation is for some of the family members to go to one event and the rest of the family, to another. Deliberate plans need to be made to maximize family togetherness. The family calendar was invented to keep track of all the directions the family was going.

Physical

The physical health of each family member needs to be reevaluated as aging progresses. Each member's nutrition, exercise, and rest needs must be reexamined.

The results of nutritional research are constantly changing making it necessary to reevaluate the family menu frequently. Cholesterol- and fat-content concerns alter meal preparation and content. Eating out poses unique problems for those on special diets while fast foods are a hazard to the health of those who constantly eat on-the-go.

13. How important does Paul say our bodies are to God in 1 Corinthians 6:19,20?

______

______

14. Read 1 Corinthians 9:25-27. What does Paul say about the importance of self-discipline and the maintenance of the body?

______

______

15. Read 1 Timothy 4:8 and note below what Paul says about physical exercise.

______

______

When W. I. Evans was dean of Central Bible College, he would say concerning this verse: "Physical exercise may profit only a little, but that little is very good." Then he would encourage the students to maintain a balanced exercise program while developing spiritually in order to be effective in the ministry.

Spiritual

The spiritual life of the family must also be assessed. Patterns of family devotions change with the growth of the children. The children's schedule of school and extracurricular activities also influences devotions. Faithfulness in church attendance and participation in church activities are essential. However, young people should not be gone from home every night of the week, even for legitimate church activities.

16. After reading John 15:9-14, write in your own words what Jesus expects His followers to do.

REDEFINING GOALS

Middle age is the appropriate time to redefine the goals of the family to incorporate the demands of moving into older adulthood.

Relationships

Aging requires adjusting to change. Flexibility is the key. The tendency in aging is to become rigid and inflexible. This temptation must be avoided and plans made for changes in housing after the last child leaves home. Later it may be appropriate to consider senior citizen housing or even nursing home placement. Plans for this must be made no later than the middle years or the family will be hard-pressed economically.

Retirement

Retirement frequently comes at the end of the midlife passage. How will you know who you are when your identity is no longer determined by your work or vocation? What will you do with your time when you don't have to report to work every morning? How will your budget have to be revised in keeping with retirement income which is usually significantly lower than in the wage-earning years?

This is when the marital relationship will be pressed. A couple that have been separated all day by work schedules for 40-plus years now find themselves together constantly. What will they do with this new time? How will they handle this forced togetherness? The wife of one newly retired man was heard to say, "Now I have too much man and not enough money!"

Avocational interests can be a salvation at this time of life. Each of the couple should be able to pursue the interests they cultivated in their younger years. It is also important that they plan specific times together, sharing in things they both enjoy.

Social

Getting involved socially with other retired persons is a good way to foster friendships, enrich social life, and expand spiritual endeavors. Many couples travel to places they did not have time to visit in their working years. Others get involved in volunteer activities and channel their energies into helping others in hospitals or nursing homes, even in nurseries, schools, and libraries.

As we become aware that some of our older friends are dying, the importance of making new, younger friendships becomes apparent. The Church needs to be active in making these opportunities available and convenient.

17. What value does Solomon place on wise counsel from a friend? (Proverbs 27:6,9).

---

18. Read Ecclesiastes 4:10. What is the ultimate value and purpose of friendship?

___

___

___

___

Leisure

It is evident that approaching older adulthood involves changes in physical stamina. This significantly influences leisure-time activities and requires creative adaptation to these changes. Less strenuous activities will need to be developed and a wider variety of interests cultivated.

Health

Since adults are living longer than a generation ago, adjustments have to be made for the extended years. Technology has made it possible for people to live longer and in better health than their parents did. Those who have not planned for these added years may see them as a curse.

Spiritual

As we approach the golden years in life, it is natural to contemplate heaven. It is important to view the end of life as the entrance into eternal life. Knowing that Jesus has gone to prepare a special place for us should inspire us to be ready to enter into His presence (John 14:1-4). As the old song says, "This world is not my home, I'm just passing through." We are like Abraham who lived in tents while seeking a city with foundations (Hebrews 11:8-10).

SUMMARY

It has been said, "Time and tide wait for no one." This is certainly true of the aging process. We know inevitable changes are coming. It is wise to anticipate these changes and not ignore or flee from them. Aging gracefully is the result of knowing who we are in Christ Jesus and inviting Him to accompany us through the passages of life.

Ask yourself: "In light of what I have studied today, what changes do I need to make in my life to complete the midlife passage successfully? What plans should I be making for a more secure future for myself and my family?"

Examine your family relationships. How can you develop a more intimate relationship with your spouse? How can you improve the relationship with your children? What about your aging parents and other family members? Does your friendship circle need to be expanded? Consider how you will wind down your career or vocation. What new leisure time activities should you be developing so you can expand your recreational life after retirement? Reevaluate your health with your family physician to ensure a healthier life in the years to come. Most important of all, take a fresh look at your relationship with God. Make sure you are ready to meet Him at any time.

LET'S REVIEW

1. What are the three steps in goal setting and how do they interact with each other?

____

____

____

2. Why should we focus more on the important than the urgent in goal setting?

____

____

3. List the six goals of midlife that should be reevaluated in making the transition into older adulthood.

1. ______________ 4. ______________

2. ______________ 5. ______________

3. ______________ 6. ______________

4. Select one of the six goals that you need to redefine while moving through the midlife passage and answer the following questions.

What *intermediate* goal should you set in order to make this transition?

____

What *short-term* goals should be made to insure that you meet the *intermediate* goal?

____

____

What *long-term* goal would result from this goal-setting strategy?______________

____

5. Reread 1 Corinthians 6:19,20. Paraphrase the passage below and personalize it. Change it from the second person (you, your) to the first person (I, my, mine)

____

____

____

STUDY 4

ILLNESS AND BODY BREAKDOWN

Physical changes are the natural result of aging. Our task is to confront these changes realistically. The story of Dorian Gray, written by Oscar Wilde, describes one man's efforts to delay the aging process. In the end, his efforts were futile.

One of the most graphic accounts of the aging process was written by Solomon as he was concluding the Book of Ecclesiastes (12:1-8). In earlier chapters he described his search for happiness while exploring the pleasures of the world. Solomon had all the earthly comforts—wisdom, wealth, power, and sensual delights. He was the wisest man of his generation, king of the most powerful kingdom in the world, possessed unlimited wealth, and had 300 wives and 700 concubines. But in his declining years he realized that his life had been meaningless.

Perpetuating Vitality

Fortunate is the person who can accept each transition of life with anticipation and live through each passage with a sense of purpose. The older we get the more important it is for us to be realistic about where we are in the life span and where we are going.

The human life span is fixed.

Research into the life potential of human cells has led to the following conclusions: (1) the length of the human life span is fixed, (2) the age at first infirmity will increase, and (3) the duration of infirmity will decrease.

There is a limit to the number of times our body cells can replicate themselves. This is called the "Hayflict Limit," named for the researcher who made the discovery. This limit appears to be an intrinsic characteristic of human cells and not the result of decay from toxic or infectious diseases. Aging is the result of functional changes within our cells rather than their inability to divide. The predicted maximum human life span has been 114 years; however, the oldest verified living person is 120 and living in France.

The age of first infirmity will increase.

Studies indicate that adults are remaining healthy for a longer period of time, Infirmity comes much later than it did for our ancestors. Only about 10 percent of adults 65 and over have a chronic health problem that restricts their major activities.

It is now estimated that a woman who celebrates her 50th birthday can expect to live another 35 to 40 years. That is equivalent to an extra adulthood passage! The good news is that she will be more healthy and less frail than women of earlier generations. As one woman was heard to say, "I'm 60 years old on paper, but in my head I'm only 45."

The man who is 65 today can expect to live at least into his early 80s. Research indicates that the longer people live, the longer they can expect to live. It is not uncommon for five generations to be living concurrently.

The duration of infirmity will decrease.

As people live longer, they do not show signs of old age until shortly before their death. Good health habits started early and sustained through middle adulthood are adding to vitality through the adult passages. A balanced, nutritious diet, adequate exercise, and sufficient rest contribute to a longer life with fewer premature diseases and accidents. The contributions of medical research, along with regular physical checkups, brighten the picture for those who maintain balanced, consistent lives.

Middle adulthood for women should not be a repeat of young adulthood. Rather, it should be a time of discovering a new attractiveness. This includes accepting a slightly thicker waist and fuller hips as natural to maturity. Increased attention to physical charms distracts from developing the inner attributes of the maturing woman. Attention to warmth and curiosity, intelligence and imagination, and wit and humor engenders more appreciation from others than trying to sustain physical beauty.

Men do not face aging as early as women, but it is inevitable. By midlife the male body does not work as efficiently as it did in the past. Because his physical prowess is waning does not mean a man is near the end of life. Midlife allows letting go of some of the outer strengths prominent in young adulthood, and encourages the discovery and nourishing of inner strengths that will sustain a man into the later years. Rather than seeking perpetual youth, midlife is a time for expanded self-discovery.

1. Read Hebrews 9:27. How does the reality of death and hope for the future help us to accept the inevitable changes which occur as we age?

Factors In Longevity

Heredity

Our genetic inheritance contributes to our longevity, but it does not determine an individual's life span. Some families are known for their long lives; others do not achieve such advanced ages. Heredity is no guarantee of long or short life—it is only one of the contributing factors. But, a person should anticipate living longer than previous generations in his or her family.

The number of years the Old Testament patriarchs lived indicates that something drastic must have happened in the atmosphere as a result of the Flood. The human life span after Noah and his sons has declined to what it is today.

2. Read Genesis 5:25-27. Compare the life span of Methuselah, the longest living person in human history, with the average life span in your family for the past three generations. Record your findings.

3. According to Psalm 90:10, what was the anticipated life span in the days of Moses? What was his observation of the quality of life in his day?

4. Describe in your own words how Solomon viewed the aging process based on Ecclesiastes 12:1-7.

____

____

____

Nutrition

Diet is important to good nutrition. Research recommends eating three balanced meals a day instead of skipping breakfast and snacking or overeating at noon. Meals should be balanced among the food groups and the portions kept within individual caloric needs.

Exercise

A half hour of vigorous exercise 3 days a week is recommended for most adults. Vigorous exercise raises the heartbeat, exercises the muscles of the heart, and fills the lower lobes of the lungs with fresh oxygen. Swimming, rapid walking (wearing the proper shoes), climbing stairs, jogging, and bicycle riding are among the recommended exercises for adults in midlife. Water aerobics are recommended for those with arthritis and other ambulatory limitations.

Sleep Patterns

Most people need more sleep than they are getting. The human body requires from 8 to 9 hours of sleep a night throughout the life span. By midlife those who cut their sleep short in adolescence and young adulthood usually have more health problems than those who maintained regular sleep patterns. Insomnia, interrupted sleep (waking up in the night and having difficulty going back to sleep), and waking up tired in the morning may indicate depression brought on by fatigue.

Lifestyle

It is important to examine the risk factors in one's lifestyle. What are you doing that would risk life or limb? Carelessness in activities leads to injury and death. Stress interferes with concentration and makes activities more dangerous than they would be under ordinary circumstances. If you are under stress, let someone else do the driving and don't engage in any activities that are beyond your skill and training.

5. Read Galatians 6:7. What principle does this Scripture give us?

____

____

____

____

____

____

What does this tell us about how we should live our lives?

____

____

____

____

____

____

____

PROCESSES OF AGING

As the years pass, our bodies change in a variety of ways. Let's examine a few.

Molecular

The aging process is called *senescence*, which refers to the deterioration in human cells and organs which begins at birth. It is encouraging to note that brain cells do not just die—they grow dormant when they are not being used. This comes from a lack of stimulation and challenge. The measured intelligence of aging adults does not begin to decrease until about 2 years before death. This decline in mental acuity is more a result of disuse than any genetic determination.

Short-term memory may deteriorate through the aging process. The vast memory banks of past events continue to expand over a lifetime and become more sophisticated through the adult years. Mentally active adults in their 80s and 90s have been known to surpass younger adults and rate near the top on psychological instruments that measure applied brain power.

Sensory

The sense of smell is often the first to dissipate. This may be followed by the sense of taste because the olfactory system contributes much to how we experience taste. Vision naturally dims with age, requiring glasses. In the later years, cataracts and glaucoma threaten sight and may require surgery.

As hearing fades, hearing aids can prolong this vital contact with the outside world. Touch will also become less acute in advanced years. Ultimately equilibrium—the sense of balance—will become less reliable.

Circulatory

One of the unmodifiable aspects of aging is arteriosclerosis, or arterial wall rigidity (hardening of the arteries). When heart valves become dysfunctional, open-heart surgery becomes the treatment of choice if angioplasty proves to be ineffective. If the brain is not adequately supplied with blood, memory loss follows, leading to dementia.

Skeletal

Bones become more brittle with age. Osteoporosis is prevalent among older women, giving them a stooped appearance. Increasing calcium intake in the younger years and exercising can help delay this degenerative process. Erect posture through the years also helps.

Care should be taken by both aging men and women to avoid falling. Broken hips are common from falls. Knee and hip replacements may extend the years of mobility in the golden years.

Endocrine

The signal that women are entering midlife is frequently the phenomenon called "menopause." This is a time for women to evaluate their physical, psychological, and spiritual condition. Women who accept the normalcy of the aging process move into a balanced and productive midlife. When the change is perceived as the end of child-bearing, it becomes a blessing rather than a curse, but some women need time to grieve the loss of fertility.

Menopause is a signal that a woman's body cannot be taken for granted. New emphasis should be placed on eating and breathing correctly as well as getting regular exercise. This is the time for planning a "time out" every day. Ruth (Mrs. Billy) Graham calls this a "spiritual tryst." She recommends a woman take an hour after lunch each day just to be a woman—soak in bubble bath, sleep, read, or listen to soothing music. It gives her the stamina to face the rest of the day when the family comes in from school and work.

Physicians tell us that almost all women experience some menopausal symptoms, but only about 10 percent have significant and potentially incapacitating problems. About 20 percent go through the process without difficulty. The remaining 70 percent are only inconvenienced by such symptoms as sadness, malaise, mild depression, irritability, and poor concentration. One woman compared it to "feeling like I am on a roller coaster." Menopause is an individualized experience—no two women experience it the same way.

Decrease in the production of the hormone estrogen leads to an increase in the rate of heart disease among women. Muscle mass begins to decrease and there is a tendency to gain weight because of sluggish metabolism. However, this can be countered by regular exercise to maintain weight at an optimal level. The loss of estrogen also greatly increases the development of osteoporosis and the appearance of facial hair.

More than 50 percent of men over age 50 experience a midlife potency crisis which may be connected to a decrease in the production of the hormone testosterone. Often men may experience an interruption in virility coincidental with their wife's going through menopause, but it need not become permanent. Male menopause is usually an "unspeakable passage." They seldom talk about it because it is devastating to their recollections of youth and is experienced with secrecy, shame, and denial. On the other hand, a report by the Massachusetts Male Aging Study found that 40 percent of normal, healthy males remained potent at age 70.

Immune System

The body's immune system is a miracle of divine creation. It is designed to fight off diseases and infections. Medical science, using herbs and plants, continues to produce compounds that form the basis for medications. God placed the herbs and plants here for us as another expression of His healing provision. Medicine, then, is as much a gift of God as the sun and rain, and other gifts of nature. When discovered and processed, prescription drugs become part of the healing process.

Society has almost eliminated premature death by eradicating 99% of the reported cases of tuberculosis, smallpox, polio, diphtheria, tetanus, typhoid and paratyphoid fevers, and whooping cough. Respiratory problems, such as pneumonia and influenza, are the major exceptions and they are only about 85% controlled. Deaths from these respiratory diseases occur almost exclusively among the infirm, the very old, or those who were already ill from another disease.

The chronic diseases that continue to be a major health hazard as aging continues include arteriosclerosis, cancer, emphysema, diabetes, osteoarthritis, and cirrhosis. These account for 80% of all premature deaths and 90% of all disabilities among older adults.

Divine Healing

It would be inappropriate to conclude a discussion of the processes of aging without reemphasizing the doctrine of divine healing. The Bible makes it clear that the God who made the body is able to heal the body and keep it healthy.

It is also wise to remember that aging is not a disease. Rather, the changes are the natural winding down of the machine we call the human body. God has promised to heal disease but not to reverse the processes of aging! However, He may choose to delay aging and even grant longer life as a province of His sovereign will, such as in the case of Hezekiah (2 Kings 20:1-11; Isaiah 38:1-8).

6. What promise did God make in Exodus 15:26 to the Children of Israel concerning healing?

____

____

____

____

What condition did the Lord give to Israel to fulfill this promise?

____

____

____

____

____

7. Read Psalm 103:2,3. What two promises did David say come from God when we praise Him? Compare this passage with James 5:15,16. How are they similar?

____

____

____

____

____

8. Why did Isaiah say the Messiah could heal our diseases? (Isaiah 53:5).

9. Read Matthew 8:16,17 and detail how Jesus fulfilled the promise of healing as predicted by Isaiah.

SUMMARY

We have attempted to explore some of the physical changes associated with midlife and offer suggestions on how to adjust to the processes of aging. We have examined some of the assumptions of medical science about perpetuating vitality and looked at some of the factors that contribute to longevity. In exploring the various aspects of aging we have discovered that there are some things we can do to prolong life and perpetuate its quality. We have also determined that some of the processes of aging are irreversible.

Finally, we have examined the promise of divine healing. May the Lord help us take seriously what we can do to prolong our quality of life so we can continue to be God's hand extended to a world that needs to know Christ, not only as Savior, but as Healer.

Let's Review

1. List the three assumptions of medical science concerning perpetuating vitality in the aging process.

2. List the five factors that contribute to longevity.

3. List six of the processes of aging.

4. Which one of the processes of aging discussed in this lesson did you find most helpful? Why was this important to you?

5. Summarize what you understand about divine healing.

Study 5

Sexual Adjustments

Why did God create sex when it has so much potential for evil? What role should sexuality play in the life of a Christian? These questions have been asked for generations by people who have seen the devastation of sexual misconduct around the world. In this study we will look at what the Bible says about human sexuality and apply it to midlife experiences.

One of the reasons God created Adam and Eve with a sexual potential was to have children and populate the earth providing caretakers for the planet. Since the Fall, humans have not only used their sexual capacity for God-ordained fulfillment, but have misused and abused the sexual drive in sinful pursuits.

Understand that sexuality refers to who you are, not to something you do. It is also essential to acknowledge that marriage was created as the only appropriate arena for sexual expression, and that the gift of sex was not limited to procreation. Adam and Eve probably enjoyed the pleasures of sexual love for some time before the birth of Cain and Abel.

Sexuality Is A Gift From God

Why was woman created? Because of the sensitivity of God to the emotional needs of man. God in relationship (Father, Son, and Holy Spirit) created humankind for relationships. Genesis 2:18 indicates that God recognized the loneliness of man without a companion. So He created woman to help meet the relational needs of man, not just to meet his sexual needs. Sex is only one of the dimensions of communication that men need.

Males and females were created separately but to be equal. Both were fashioned in the image of God. Genesis 1:27 says that God created man in His own image. The generic use of the word "man" is employed here to include both male and female. It was only after Adam and Eve were created that the whole of creation was declared to be "very good" (Genesis 1:31).

The second chapter of Genesis describes the two-stage process of human creation. Man was custom-made by the hand of God from the dust of the earth He had spoken into existence in the initial stages of creation (Genesis 2:7). Later, woman was taken out of the side of man (Genesis 2:21,22). In the original text rib means hunk, which indicates God took not only skeletal material, but also circulatory, neurological, muscle and fatty tissue, and skin with which He constructed the female body. Then Adam and Eve were introduced to each other and instructed to become one flesh (Genesis 2:24).

God made it clear that when a couple marry they are to disengage from enmeshment with their families of origin and establish their own home. Again in Genesis 2:24 the generic form of "man" is used to mean humankind. Both the bride and groom are to leave their mother and father and cling to their marriage partner. This leaving is to be psychological and emotional as well as geographic so they can be free to establish a new home under the sovereignty of God.

1. Read Genesis 1:1 to 2:25 in several versions of the Bible. Using your own words write your observations concerning the creation of man and woman.

____

____

____

____

____

____

Sexual relations are appropriate only within marriage. God's plan for sexual expression is specific. Celibacy before marriage. Virginity at the time of marriage. Monogamy during marriage. Celibacy after marriage is terminated by either death or divorce until the survivor remarries.

This, then, precludes fornication (premarital sex), adultery (extramarital sex), incest (sex among family members), homosexuality (same gender sexual relations), and bestiality (sex with animals, also called zoophilia). If everyone followed God's injunctions, all of the sexually transmitted diseases in the world—including AIDS—would be wiped out in one generation!

2. After reading Leviticus 18:20; 20:10; Matthew 5:27; 15:19; 1 Corinthians 6:9,15-18; 1 Timothy 1:10, list below what the Bible teaches about premarital and extramarital sex.

3. What does God's Word teach about incest? (Leviticus 18:6-18; 20:11,12,14,17,19-21; 1 Corinthians 5:1).

4. Read Genesis 19:1-11; Leviticus 18:22; 20:13; Romans 1:24-27; 1 Corinthians 6:9. What does Scripture say about homosexuality?

5. What do Exodus 22:19 and Leviticus 18:23; 20:15,16 say about bestiality (zoophilia)?

6. Read Hebrews 13:4 and record what the New Testament writer says about the sanctity of marriage.

Christian marriage was designed by God to be an egalitarian relationship—one of equality. This includes both privileges and responsibilities.

7. What does Paul say in 1 Corinthians 7:1-7 regarding who should initiate sexual relations in marriage?

What does Paul say is the only reason to interrupt the love-making cycle in marriage?

8. Read Ephesians 5:21. What does Paul say about mutual submission of husband to wife and wife to husband?

9. In light of Galatians 3:28, how does Paul compare the equality of husband and wife with other interpersonal relationships?

Scripture shows that God has designed two sources of passion in the life of the married believer: (1) your relationship with God and (2) your relationship with your spouse. Therefore, it is important for a husband and wife to maintain an active devotional life and seek to grow closer to the Lord every day, both individually and as a couple. The closer you are to God, the more intimate your relationship will be with each other.

Purposes Of Sex In Marriage

Loving Expression

God created sex as the most intimate way a husband and wife can express their love.

10. What does Genesis 2:25 say about Adam and Eve in their primal state?

11. How does Genesis 24:67 describe Isaac's attitude toward Rebekah when he first met her?

___

___

___

During sex, love is expressed verbally and nonverbally. Studies suggest that men are more stimulated by what they see and women are more influenced by what they hear. On the verbal level, the couple express in words their love, appreciation, affection, and admiration for each other. Such expressions are stimulating to both the mind and body. But, they require total honesty.

12. How does Ephesians 4:15 apply to expressing love in an intimate relationship?

___

___

___

Mutual Pleasure

God's intent for sexual expression in marriage to be a pleasurable experience is a theme running through the Bible. Sex is one of the most powerful of our God-given drives. Not only is it to be enjoyed—it must be disciplined. Sex in marriage was not designed to be compulsive; rather, it is to be expressive. It is a time when a couple communicate, "I love you with every fiber of my being," in a way that words can never convey. One only has to read the Song of Songs to see the beauty of sexual love. Paul picks up the theme and compares marital love to the mystical relationship between Christ and the Church. And, Paul writes that this attitude of oneness with Christ and each other is part of our Christian witness.

13. What was Isaac's attitude toward physical displays of affection as outlined in Genesis 26:7-11? How would this type of activity strengthen a marriage?

___

___

___

Tension Reduction

God created the sexual drive as a way of releasing tensions that build up in a day. One of the reasons for Paul's instructions in 1 Corinthians 7:1-7 is to make both husband and wife sensitive to the sexual needs of the other. Research has verified that sexual intercourse is a natural sedative which is an antidote to insomnia. Mutually releasing the normal tensions of the day becomes an act of love, not just fulfilling a selfish desire. Paul was very aware of the sensual temptations in a secular society and pointed out the necessity of meeting sexual needs at home.

Perpetuate Humanity

In Genesis 1:28 God gave the first couple two assignments to carry out on earth:

The first assignment was to bear children. To populate the earth was the first commandment God gave to Adam and Eve. Through proper discipline, humankind is responsible in its role of replenishing the earth. A self-disciplined couple will plan for only as many children as they can successfully feed, clothe, and educate.

Secondly, the couple was assigned to maintain environmental control. This command of God was to keep the biosphere of earth a balanced ecological system. Again, a disciplined and concerted effort is required in maintaining the ecological balance of the earth to make it a fit place for our children and grandchildren to live. Thus we should fulfill the first two commandments God gave to humankind—even before the Decalogue.

Marital Celebration

Sexual intercourse between a Christian couple in the presence of God becomes an act of worship—a celebration. God, the creator of sexual communication, is present at each act of love and turns it into a spiritual experience when our hearts are right with Him and with each other. Of this holy occasion Dwight Small says in *Christian: Celebrate Your Sexuality*: "Sexuality is an expression of the whole person; it belongs to the symphony of human existence. It cannot be compartmentalized, but is the music of the body, complete with rhythms and melodies and harmonies. Throughout the relationship of marriage there plays, as it were, the obbligato of sexual love."

SEXUAL ADJUSTMENTS IN MIDLIFE

As one encounters midlife, a number of sexual challenges may arise. Let's examine a few.

Inhibited Desire

Some men experience a lowering of their sex drive in midlife. Whether impotence is cause or effect is debatable. Impotence can result from smoking, which inhibits the blood flow to the genital organs; prolonged alcohol consumption, which kills the nerves needed to sustain an erection; and diet, which allows high cholesterol levels to clog the arteries. Lowered production of the male hormone testosterone and increased levels of stress also interfere with sexual functioning. Medications for hypertension (high blood pressure) and high cholesterol contribute to impotence in the male which interferes with intercourse.

Inhibited desire in the female may be the result of guilt feelings that arise from lack of information concerning her own sexuality. It can also be a residual of sexual abuse in childhood. It is also possible that the decrease of estrogen accompanying menopause can contribute to intercourse being painful.

Sexual Disorders

Premature ejaculation in the male and vaginismus in the female are treatable disorders. Homosexuality and transvestitism (cross-dressing) are other disorders that require professional attention.

Physiological Changes

Menopause has been called the "death of youth" in women. It begins near the end of young adulthood and continues through the early stages of middle adulthood.

Menopause is not a disease that can be avoided or treated—it is a universal physiological phenomenon that is experienced differently by each woman.

This is a time for women to evaluate where they are physically, psychologically, and spiritually. If they recognize and accept what their body is telling them, they can expect a more balanced, productive midlife. Mood swings may bring sadness, malaise, mild depression, irritability, and poor concentration. The good news is that once a woman has traversed the menopausal passage she can forget fears of pregnancy and monthly mood swings.

New research suggests there is a male menopause which is accompanied by a midlife male potency crisis. In England it is called viropause and on the European continent it is called andropause. And it is just that, a pause in virility and vitality that does not need to be a permanent condition. It appears that what happens to men in the change of life is more gradual than what their wives experience in menopause.

Statistics indicate that more than half of the men over 50 have sexual problems of some kind. The crisis can be exacerbated by emotional upheavals such as loss of a job, the last child leaving home, premature death of a spouse, or an impending divorce. Physical symptoms include gradual decrease in muscle mass and strength, increase in body fat, and hormonal changes that bring interrupted sleep, lethargy, depression, irritability, nervousness, difficulty concentrating, memory lapses, and mood swings. Circulatory symptoms include numbness, tingling in arms and legs, headaches, dizzy spells, and night sweats.

Male sexual function ebbs with age and the frequency of impotence increases with age. On the other hand, 40 percent of normal, healthy males remain completely potent at age 70, some into their 80s if they have an understanding wife.

Emotional Problems

One of the major sources of sexual problems in midlife is pornography. The Greek word for fornication is *porneia* which means "sex for sale." This is where we get our word *pornography*. The use of visual media as stimulation for sexual fantasy or activity is damaging to mind, body, and soul. It is using the image of another person vicariously for sexual indulgence. The memory of a pornographic image hangs like a ghost over the marriage bed.

Another problem is sexual affairs. Adultery is committed when a married person has sexual relations with another person of the complementary sex to whom he/she is not married.

Adultery means taking sexual stimulation from a spouse and sharing it with someone else. This breaks the marriage vow and violates the laws of God. An affair doesn't have to involve intercourse to be adultery. Anytime a person spends time, energy, money, or attention on sexual things outside of marriage it is adultery. It may be called emotional or spiritual attraction, but it is wrong and indefensible.

14. Read Matthew 5:27,28. What implication does this Scripture have for a believer regarding marital fidelity?

____

____

____

____

____

The threat of divorce is extremely traumatic to midlife happiness. When couples are in marital crisis, it is wise for them to seek counseling to work on conflict resolution. Divorce was never God's idea. It was only allowed because of the hardness of the human heart in Moses' day. It must be remembered, however, that God loves the person who is the victim of divorce.

15. What is God's attitude toward divorce as stated in Malachi 2:16?

16. What is Jesus' position on divorce? (Mark 10:1-12).

Empty Nest

Although it is expected, children leaving home create a vacuum that puts emotional strain on a marriage. When the children leave, couples who have maintained an intimate relationship and continued to keep romance in their marriage have a much easier time than those couples who invested more energy in the children than they did in their marital relationship.

One of the best ways to prepare for the emancipation of children is to go back and reread Genesis 2:24. Whom could Adam and Eve leave? They had just been created. This command is prophetic. Before the first child arrived in the home of the first family, God tried to prepare the parents to help their children leave home and cleave to their new spouse. Couples who participate in this emancipation will be happier.

SUMMARY

In our attempt to explore what the Bible says about human sexuality, we have discovered that sex originated in the mind of God. It is His gift to be received with anticipation and guarded with integrity. We have examined the purposes of sex in marriage and discovered new freedoms in expressing our sexuality in Christian marriage. Then, to apply what we discovered to the midlife experience, we have looked at some of the sexual adjustments that may be necessary in the midlife passage. In doing so, we have focused on the goodness of God in creating sex for the expression of physical love in marriage and examined some of the emotional ramifications that result from not using this gift as God intended. We then looked at how parents can assist maturing children in making the transition from home to become fully functioning individuals.

Let's Review

1. How does the Bible view sex within marriage?

2. Based on Scripture support the statement: "Marriage was created to be an egalitarian relationship."

3. List five purposes of sex in marriage.

4. What physiological changes have the greatest impact on men and women moving from young adulthood into midlife?

5. What impact does pornography have on marriage?

6. What did you discover in this study that you think will assist you in your own midlife passage?

STUDY 6

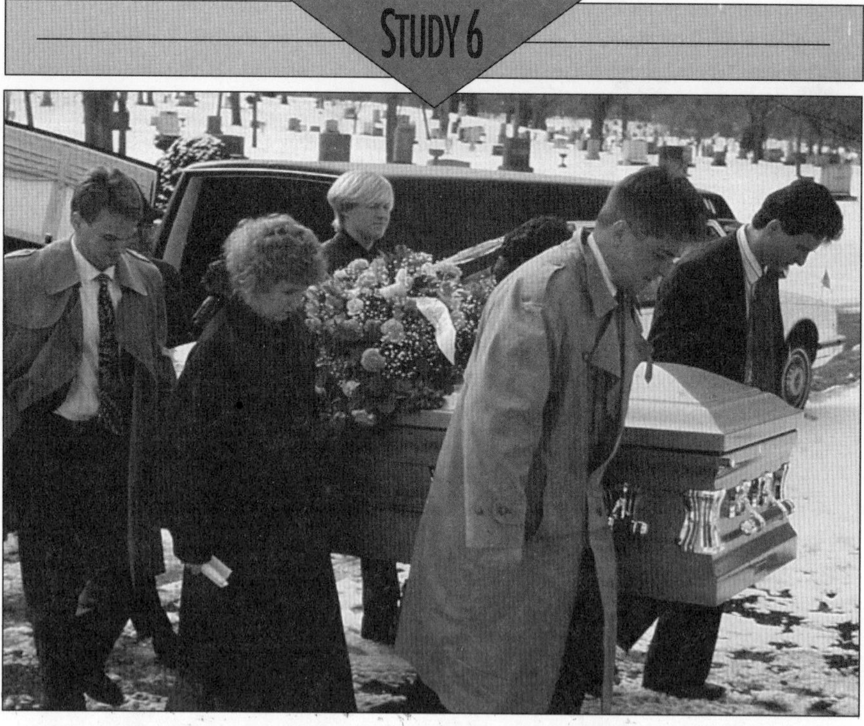

FACING MORTALITY

Death begins with life. From the time we are born, the cells in our bodies begin to die and new ones are constantly being formed. Ultimately, if accident or disease does not hasten the process, the cycle stops through the normal processes of aging and we die. This fact is quite different from the Pennsylvania Dutch proverb which states: "Death will come to thee and to thee, but not to me!" Hebrews 9:27 is both a promise and an ultimatum—death is inevitable.

We do not have a choice as to when we will die or how, but we do have control over how we will face death and where we will spend eternity. In this study we want to learn how to comprehend and to face the inevitability of death and to reaffirm the hope we have of spending eternity with our Lord and Savior Jesus Christ.

Perspectives On Death

A cursory look at the obituary column in the daily newspaper reveals that people of all ages die, not just the elderly. It brings home the truth that the cause of death is as varied as the number of individuals involved. A person's obituary also gives a summary statement of what that person thought was important in life. How do you want your obituary to read? What do you want included in your eulogy? What do you want on your tombstone?

Views of death in ancient history.

The ancient Egyptians believed in life after death. They perfected the art of mummification to preserve the body and built huge pyramids as burial places for their rulers. Slaves were buried alive in the tombs of the pharaohs so they could serve their masters in their afterlife. The ancient Egyptians fervently believed that the body would be resuscitated after death, but was destined to an unknown existence.

The Greeks accepted death as inevitable, but had no hope for life after death. Theirs was an agnostic view that said, "Nobody still alive knows what happens after death. The dead may, but dead men tell no tales." The philosopher Socrates believed that death was a great liberator; it loosened the soul from its prison in the body which then went back to its eternal home. But he knew nothing about that home. Plato, a student of Socrates, taught that the body disintegrated after death but the soul lived forever, ultimately coming back to earth in reincarnation. This view was and is shared by numerous contemporary African tribes and Eastern religions.

Two conflicting views of death were sustained in ancient Rome. Cicero said, "After death we shall for the first time really live." On the other hand, the politician Galus said, "Beyond this life there is no place for either trouble or joy." It was into this culture of contradictions that Christ came.

Judeo-Christian concepts of death.

Jesus presented an alternative to the pessimistic view of the ancient Mediterranean world. Drawing from the Old Testament Scriptures, Jesus referred to the person as an integrated whole. The heart, soul, and might of Deuteronomy 6:4-6 were aspects of this integrated whole person.

The presence of death in the world was an inevitable event which represents the cessation of natural life. Death, which brought a release from pain, was no respecter of persons and came to the young and the old.

1. Read Genesis 3:17-19. Why did death come into human history?

____

____

2. According to Joshua 23:14, what was the source of Joshua's confidence as he faced the end of his life?

____

____

____

3. Read Psalm 116:15. How does God view the death of His saints?

The Old Testament concept of resurrection was brought into the New Testament in the teachings of Jesus. He laid the foundation from which the apostles drew to illustrate the implications of death for both the believer and the unbeliever. In the New Testament, death is pictured as a laying aside of the body or the taking down of the tent of a temporary pilgrimage from which the spirit has departed (2 Corinthians 5:1). Death is in the world because of sin, and comes to everyone.

4. Based on Daniel 12:2, what was Daniel's view of death?

5. What did Paul teach about death in Romans 6:23?

Jesus indicated that no correlation can be drawn between the manner of a person's death and the quality of his/her life (Matthew 5:45; Luke 13:1-5). New Testament Christians maintained hope in life after death as was illustrated by the martyrs of the first century. To them, death was a glorious experience leading to union with God.

6. Read 1 Corinthians 15:17-19. What did Paul teach about the resurrection and life after death?

Contemporary views of death.

Ours is a death-denying culture. Many people act as though they believe death will never come to them. We isolate the dying by consigning them to sterile hospital rooms and punish them by staying away from them in their final days. We avoid touching them when we know death is coming and condescendingly visit them in their terminal hours. When we try to forget the dead, we are only haunted by them. This secular view of death is inconsistent with an awareness that Christ is Lord of both life and death.

Dr. Elizabeth Kubler-Ross, who has spent most of her professional career dealing with dying patients, says that our unconscious never really accepts the idea of death occurring naturally. The end of life must be attributed to some malicious outside intervention. It is inconceivable that we should die of natural causes or old age—we can only be killed, she concluded.

Death anxiety is different from general anxiety. It is accompanied by a sense of helplessness and a fear of the unknown that comes when a person has not been able to discover meaning in life. Committed Christians who have found meaning in life do not experience death anxiety.

7. After reading 1 Kings 19:1-5, note below how Elijah reacted to Jezebel's threat to kill him.

____

____

THE REALITY OF DEATH

Death comes to all and is a normal event that terminates life as we know it on earth. It may be viewed either as the last enemy or as the friend who ushers us into the presence of God. John Quincy Adams, fifth president of the United States, was asked how he was one day. The 80-year-old statesman replied: "John Quincy Adams is quite well. But the house where he lives is becoming dilapidated. It is tottering. Time and the seasons have nearly destroyed it and it is becoming quite uninhabitable. I shall move out soon. But John Quincy Adams is quite well, thank you."

8. What did Paul believe about death and the resurrection as recorded in 1 Thessalonians 4:13-17?

____

____

____

Death is a personal event. Death is a reality which each person must face. For death is not something that happens to us—it is an event in which we must participate. How we face this terminal event becomes our statement to the world as to the quality of our lives and the destiny for which we have prepared.

Death is a social event. Usually, death occurs within a community of friends and relatives (occasionally strangers) who assess whether the event is a defeat or a victory. This is why the Christian community should be active in ministering both to the dying and to the survivors who are struggling with grief.

9. Read Genesis 49:1,33. In what kind of setting did Jacob die?

____

____

The mystery of death lies in our inability to comprehend what the death of the self means. Many protect themselves by avoiding its reality. Some researchers think it is impossible to contemplate "nonbeing," so a person seldom believes in his or her own death. As a result, on the unconscious level most people are convinced of their immortality.

10. What does Paul say about the mystery of death as recorded in 1 Corinthians 15:51-53?

Death is a liberating event. Pain may precede death, but death actually brings an end to pain and anxiety. The fear of death, beyond the consciousness of sin, lies in guilt, loneliness, and fear of the unknown, which are not Christian concerns. Therefore, death liberates the believer from emotions that complicate the death of unbelievers.

For the intrinsically motivated Christian, death frees us from pain and fear. It transports us to another plane of existence to await the resurrection in the presence of God in heaven.

11. Read Psalm 23:4. What was David's concept of death?

FACING DEATH

After years of working with dying patients, Dr. Kubler-Ross has identified five stages which the dying go through in the death process.

Denial

Following the shock of hearing that one is dying, the normal reaction is denial. "No, it can't be me! You must have made some mistake." Denial can be useful when it allows the dying person time to develop skills for coping with the reality of impending death.

Anger

The anger may be directed at the physician because he or she brought the bad news, toward God for letting the illness or accident happen, or to the survivors because they will continue to live. Anger allows the patient to look for the cause of this "punishment," which is usually based on the universal concept that death is malicious and capricious. The anger will subside more quickly when the patient is allowed to express the emotion without restraints from others.

Bargaining

As the anger subsides, bargaining sets in. This involves negotiating for another chance at life.

12. According to 2 Kings 20:1-6, how did Hezekiah react to the word that he was going to die?

____

____

In bargaining, the patient promises to do a better job of living if time is extended. Not all patients bargain, however. Those who have an intrinsic relationship with the Lord Jesus Christ move to the anticipation of going home to heaven, for they are ready to die. They see death as the entrance into eternal life.

Depression

Depending on the person's view of life and life after death, the depression may be intense or only a blue mood. This depression comes from realizing that disability and weakness can no longer be ignored and must be squarely faced with eternity in view. Depression is also evident in the sadness that comes from impending separation from the world and those we love.

Acceptance

This is a time to make sure all personal affairs are in order—the will current, funeral planned, and burial arrangements completed. Acceptance is the final stage of rest before death. It is the appropriate time to say good-bye to the world, our families, and our loved ones. Acceptance culminates in a wish to die since the patient will have successfully detached from the world and its responsibilities. Death becomes a great relief.

Through these five stages runs the thread of hope—hope for a miraculous healing, for the discovery of a new medication or medical intervention that will extend life. That is why we continue to pray for the sick even when the prognosis of the physician is foreboding.

13. Read Job 19:25-27 and note how Job expressed his acceptance of death and its aftermath.

____

____

____

Friends and family go through the same emotional stages as the dying patient, experiencing denial, anger, bargaining, and depression before they move on to accept the inevitable.

14. Read 2 Samuel 1:11,12. How did David respond to the news that King Saul was dead?

____

____

____

 **15. Read John 11:17-22. What was Martha's reaction to the death of Lazarus?**

____

____

Experiencing Bereavement

There are a variety of ways people experience bereavement. Let's look at a few.

Mourning

Mourning is the process of accepting the reality of death. It is an anxiety that involves recouping from the loss and reestablishing an appropriate lifestyle. Mourning allows the survivor to disengage psychologically from the loss by reviewing the past and the significance of the relationship that cannot be reestablished.

Grieving

Mourning gives way to grieving as the healing process continues. Grieving is a healthy process and essential to recovery from loss. It involves both cognitive and emotional reevaluation.

Normal Grief

Normal grief is different from depression. Grief involves sadness but is free from the guilt or shame that characterize depression. While grief leads to a temporary withdrawal from normal daily activities and is preoccupied with the deceased person, it is short-term and seldom leads to serious psychological upheavals.

 **16. How did Solomon view grief in Ecclesiastes 3:4?**

____

____

Abnormal Grief

Abnormal reactions to grief come in three forms.

Chronic grief is seen when the bereaved person prolongs grief reactions along with shame, guilt, and self-blame. In chronic grief the survivor either partially identifies with the deceased person or develops aggressive behaviors to mask the prolonged pain.

 **17. Read 1 Samuel 16:1. How did God view Samuel's prolonged grief?**

____

____

Inhibited grief displays itself when the normal responses to grief are tempered by the substitution of other behaviors that mask the grief process. This person is in denial and disowns the pain of grieving by proceeding with business as usual.

Delayed grief involves repression of grief reactions for weeks, months, or even years. It resembles chronic grief but surfaces long after the death of the loved one.

To grieve over the death of a loved one is normal. It is not a weakness and does not indicate a lack of Christian faith. The bereaved person should not only be allowed to grieve, but should be encouraged to express grief in a natural, healthy way. It is a task that must be worked through individually. Since death is not the ultimate tragedy, the believer's grief is different from the grief of those who have no hope.

18. According to 1 Thessalonians 4:13, how is the grief of the Christian different from that of the unbeliever?

____

____

____

It is estimated that it takes a minimum of 2 years to grieve over the death of a spouse. It may be another 2 or 3 years before a person is sufficiently free from attachment to consider marrying again. (This is also true in divorce recovery.)

The crucial difference between the mourning and grief of the believer and the unbeliever is that Christians do not have to go through the experience alone. We know the Lord will be with us. It is good to remind ourselves that nothing comes into the life of the believer without the presence of the Father.

19. Read Isaiah 53:3,4. What has Jesus done for us to help us handle grief and sorrow?

____

____

20. How can the promises in Hebrews 2:14; 4:14-16, help us in times of loss and grief?

____

____

SUMMARY

We have faced the reality of death and noted that the Bible offers us eternal hope in Christ Jesus. We looked at how death and dying were viewed in ancient Egypt, Greece, Rome, and in biblical times. We have noted that the current view of death in the Western world is basically denial and anxiety. Since these are not Christian concerns, we have examined the dimensions of death and the difference between the view of the world and the view of the Christian.

In looking at how to face death and experience bereavement, we have turned to biblical principles that will help us when death strikes and we are plunged into mourning. Certainly, the Bible is filled with hope for such inevitable events.

LET'S REVIEW

1. Contrast the views of death in ancient Egypt, Greece, and Rome.

2. Basically, what is the Judeo-Christian view of death?

3. List five ways in which the reality of death can be personalized.

4. Through what five stages does a person go when facing death according to Kubler-Ross?

5. How does God's comfort help the Christian face mourning and grief?

Study 7

The Sandwich Years

The sandwich years are among the most perplexing of the life span. Your children are still looking to you for attention and guidance but your aging parents are now looking to you to sustain them during their declining years. You are caught in the middle. Recent studies have revealed that the average woman in midlife can expect to spend more years caring for her or her husband's parents than she did caring for her own children.

Do you spend time with your aging parents to the neglect of your growing children? Do you spend time with your children to the neglect of your aging parents? In the process, do you neglect your marriage? Do you neglect your work which you must sustain in order to be able to meet the financial demands of the three family units that are depending on you for what seems to be EVERYTHING? More importantly, do you neglect yourself?

In this study we will learn to apply biblical principles for handling the pressures that come from being responsible for both growing children and aging parents.

Crisis Management In The Family

The Chinese language has a wonderful way of describing a crisis. As a pictographic language, the Chinese use pictures to convey the meaning of words. The Chinese word for crisis consists of two word pictures. The first figure is for challenge. The second figure is for opportunity. And that is exactly what a family crisis is—a challenge accompanied by an opportunity.

1. Read Psalm 37:1-8. What does David suggest an individual do in place of worrying?

____

____

____

2. Compare Proverb 3:5,6 with Psalm 37:3. What are some practical ways of using this information to address the perplexities of life?

____

____

____

3. On the basis of the promises found in Deuteronomy 31:6 and Hebrews 13:5,6, what confidence can we have when we face a crisis in our family?

____

____

____

4. According to James 3:17, how can we recognize the wisdom that comes from heaven?

____

____

____

H. Norman Wright suggests there are four components to a family crisis.

A Hazardous Event

A chain of events that culminate by getting everyone's attention. One of the children, either consciously or unconsciously, does something out of the ordinary to get the attention of the family. It may be failing grades in school, an unwanted pregnancy, or a run-in with the law. Or an aging parent suffers a medical emergency which demands immediate attention.

A Vulnerable State

In response to the crisis, one or both of the midlife parents are in a vulnerable emotional state and their defenses are low. Lack of sleep, stress on the job, too many demands from too many directions—all exhaust the coping mechanisms of parents who have their own midlife challenges.

A Precipitating Factor

This is the "straw that broke the camel's back." Since emotions are cumulative, little stresses build up until there are no reserves on which to draw. Then the confrontation is out of proportion to the actual event.

A State Of Active Crisis

The midlife parent displays symptoms of anxiety brought on by stress. Emotional reserves are low and he or she overreacts to the situation. Feelings of helplessness are magnified as relief is sought. This is a time of lowered mental and emotional efficiency accompanied by panic.

Resolving a crisis has four phases as well.

The Impact Phase

This is a brief period of time in which parents feel the full impact of the crisis. Since the whole family is impacted by the new set of circumstances, the parents deal with the crisis appropriately. They must take charge of the crisis, so they need to draw on spiritual strength to sustain them.

The Confusion Phase

Since midlife parents cannot follow the natural tendency to withdraw from the situation, the temptation to flee must be countered by a determination to see the crisis through. This involves listening carefully to the child or elderly parent who precipitated the crisis.

The Adjustment Phase

This period of time allows for adjustments to the crisis and its aftermath. Fears are replaced by facts as the equilibrium of the family is reestablished.

The Reconciliation Phase

Hope begins to surface with a new perspective on life. New strengths emerge as new values for approaching life are devised. This is when change leads to exciting growth. The family will survive—but in a changed condition.

A person's attitude in a crisis determines whether it becomes a restricting, crippling tragedy or a growth-producing experience in spite of the pain. Rather than trying to reestablish old norms, new and innovative ways of coping must be devised.

Responsibilities To Growing Children

Individuation is the process by which a child withdraws from dependence on parents and starts to develop his/her own identity. It usually begins around age 2 when the child wants to do things for himself or herself. When you try to tie shoe laces, or button or snap clothing, the child slaps your hand away and says, "Let me do." This is a golden moment. It is the first signal that the child is intent on becoming a fully functioning human being.

5. What does Solomon say in Proverbs 22:6 about the child who is consistently taught attitudes and values to live by?

This process continues to develop with the child accepting more responsibility until the independence of adolescence is achieved. When the individual completes high school he or she starts demonstrating responsible behavior. This is confirmed in delay of gratification. The teenager does not expect to have what he or she wants on demand but is willing to save for purchases and complete work assignments before realizing play and leisure time.

Emancipation is when late teens or young adults are ready to move out on their own. They are now able to enter the workforce and earn an income sufficient to maintain a car and an apartment.

Fortunate is the maturing adult who emancipates before marriage. He or she will have a period of single living before taking on the responsibilities of marriage and family.

The key behavior at this point is interdependence. The person matures beyond the independence of adolescence and shares with his or her parents in ways that sustain independence while maintaining a loving and caring relationship. This mutual sharing with parents indicates a successful disengagement from the family of origin and the transition to a fully functioning adult. They are now ready for marriage and establishing a home.

6. Read Matthew 21:28-31. How did both of the sons in the parable show they were still not ready for adulthood?

---

7. How can adopting the attitude expressed by Paul in 1 Corinthians 11:1 assist parents in helping their growing children become interdependent?

A new phenomenon developed as the 20th century grew to a close. The workplace became so unstable that many young people who struck out on their own became frustrated in their efforts and moved back home with their parents. These young adults who returned home in an attempt to stabilize their lives parallel the prodigal son whom Jesus described.

8. How do we know the younger son tried to emancipate before he was ready? Read Luke 15:11-24.

How did the older brother show he was as immature as his younger brother had been?

Responsibilities To Aging Parents

Studies indicate that the majority of adults over 60 are quite able to function independently. Only about 10 percent of adults over 65 have a chronic health problem that interferes with their independence. As a result, aging parents are better off living in their own home rather than with their children or in a retirement community. A sense of independence contributes to longevity and happiness in the aging population. This is so even when it is necessary to bring in nursing help periodically to care for specific illnesses and to arrange for meals. Aging parents need frequent interaction with their children and grandchildren. They also need to be visited by their friends and neighbors.

Couples in the sandwich generation are faced with the choice of spending their limited financial resources on their aging parents or saving for their own retirement. Many women in midlife have been expected to do the work of unpaid caregiver to the disabled elderly, usually in their own homes. It is not unusual for women in their 60s and 70s to be caring for parents in their 90s.

When parents need more care than is available in their own home or with their children, retirement placement becomes necessary. It is important for the family to look for quality facilities that meet the social, emotional, and physical needs of the aging parents.

Children involved in this selection process should prepare a list of guidelines to insure that their parents will receive the assistance they need at an affordable price. This is not always an easy task, but it is essential to the well-being of the whole family. Retirement home living should offer as much freedom of movement as possible with adequate nursing supervision of medications and provision for regular, balanced meals.

9. Read Mark 7:10-13. How does Jesus regard our responsibility to our aging parents?

When one or both of the aging parents requires more care and supervision than a retirement community offers, a convalescent facility or nursing home is the next option. Usually the family has time to make a studied selection of this facility, unless an accident occurs. It is extremely important that medical care and supervision be adequate so the needs of the parent(s) can be met on a 24-hour basis.

A relatively new option for families is available through the hospice movement. This is a place where terminally ill patients can receive quality care from trained personnel in a homelike setting. The hospice movement has expanded greatly since the advent of the AIDS epidemic. However, it is not limited to persons with AIDS.

The hospice is designed to accommodate any patient in the final stages of life. The personnel are trained as much in compassion as they are in medicine and can make the final days of a person as fulfilling as their circumstances permit. There are no illusions here. Everyone knows that death is the next step and assistance is given in making that last transition with dignity in a loving community.

10. After reading Ephesians 6:1-3, identify below God's command for children in relationship to their parents.

____

____

____

____

What reason does He give for this expectation?

____

____

____

11. Read Ephesians 5:33 in conjunction with Ephesians 6:2. Where do children learn honor?

____

____

____

____

What promise was given to children who honor their parents?

____

____

____

12. Read Genesis 2:24, Matthew 19:5, and Ephesians 5:31. When are adult children released from the command to obey their parents in the daily aspects of their lives?

13. Reread Mark 7:10-13 and Ephesians 6:3. When are adult children released from honoring their parents?

MAINTAINING BALANCE

Managing career demands along with responsibilities to growing children and aging parents requires delicate balance. It is a special problem for the woman who is expected to care for aging parents in her own home. An estimated 90 percent of the caregivers of aging adults are women who are not paid for their services.

One survey estimated that 21 percent of the women caretakers of the elderly quit jobs paying an average of $29,400 a year to spend up to 18 hours a day caring for elderly parents for no pay at all. Because they dropped out of their careers in their peak earning years, many of these women will be impoverished in their own older adulthood.

Each person making the transition from midlife into the third adulthood is faced with a choice between passive aging and successful aging—"growing old gracefully." Successful aging requires that the adult prepare for a meaningful old age by thoroughly enjoying the next 20 to 30 years.

Successful aging requires a commitment to continuing self-development and striving to accomplish any unrealized goals. Instead of calling it aging, Gail Sheehy suggests we call it *sageing*, the process by which men and women continue to accumulate wisdom and become the sages of the contemporary culture, much like the seers of biblical times.

If current trends continue, most of us will live much longer than we have been led to believe. That is why it is important for us to take care of our bodies and minds so they will be healthy in the later years.

In this period of life people should develop a daily discipline of mental exercise. It is better to be active and read your Bible or even the newspaper than to watch

TV passively. Regular Bible study, working crossword puzzles, keeping journals, balancing your checkbook, keeping up with the stock market, and reading the fine print on insurance forms are all positive ways of keeping the mind stimulated.

Exercise, such as long daily walks that oxygenate sluggish blood, energizes the body to release the body's natural mood-elevating endorphins. This produces the positive attitude that is like medicine (Proverbs 17:22). This signals your immune system that life is worth fighting for. Research indicates that we never get too old to profit from exercise.

The secret of surviving the sandwich generation is to increase intimacy in your marriage throughout your life span. This involves sharing and caring on all levels of the relationship: mentally, emotionally, spiritually, and physically. Postmenopausal couples can explore physical intimacy without fears of pregnancy and learn to maximize their sexual and emotional closeness. Rather than fearing dying, this is the time to develop a relationship worth living for.

14. Read Ephesians 5:21,22,25,28,33 and Colossians 3:18-21 and list the guidelines given in these verses which would help increase intimacy in a marriage.

____

____

____

____

____

____

____

____

____

____

SUMMARY

In this study we have looked at biblical ways of handling pressures between growing children and aging parents. We have examined crisis management in the family and traced some of the responsibilities parents have to their growing children.

Then we looked at our responsibilities to our aging parents and explored different steps in providing adequately for them as they grow older. Finally, we considered how to maintain balance in this paradoxical period of life.

In the process we have discovered that God's Word can help adults in midlife face the conflicting challenges of the sandwich generation. Fortunately, the promise of Scripture is still ours to claim (Hebrews 13:8; 1 John 4:4).

LET'S REVIEW

1. What are the component parts of a family crisis?

2. Distinguish between dependence, independence, and interdependence in the maturing of children.

3. What are the progressive steps in providing housing for aging parents?

4. How can the family balance career demands with the demands of growing children and aging parents?

5. What are some of the ways you can increase intimacy in your midlife marriage?

STUDY 8

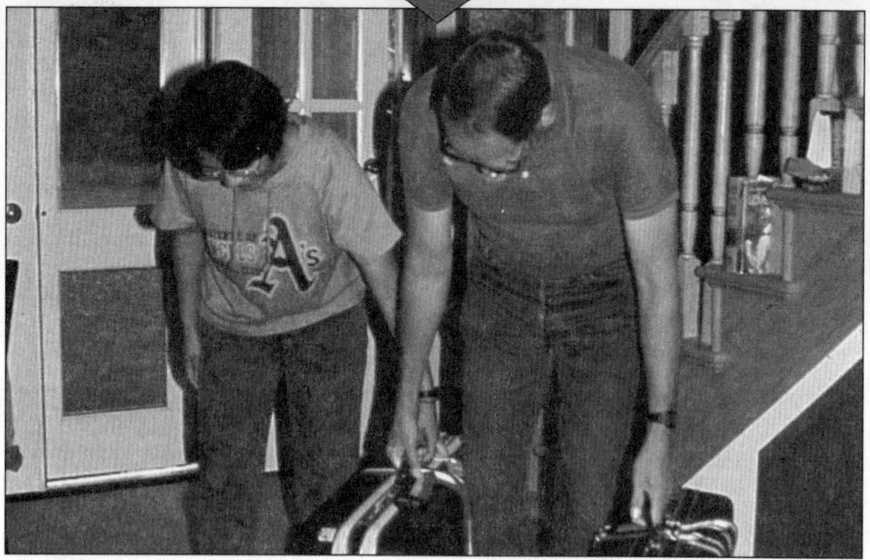

PREPARING FOR THE EMPTY NEST

There is life after children! This is good news for those who have prepared adequately for their child-free years. However, those who don't let their children grow up are in for a rude awakening.

We are going to look at ways of adjusting to life after the children leave home and discover ways to find happiness in the passage through the midlife. Couples should develop their relationship through the childbearing years and child-rearing period. Parents who have kept their romance alive will find midlife an exciting passage.

It is never too late to focus on the marriage relationship. Rather than distracting from the quality of family life, children find assurance in knowing that their parents are going to stay together and continue to grow in their relationship. Numerous surveys have yielded a constant statistic: the most important gift a father can give his children is to demonstrate his love for their mother (Ephesians 5:33).

Life After Children

Planning for a life together after the children are grown should begin early in the marriage, before the first child is born. Couples need to start looking for ways to say, "I love you," from the beginning of their relationship. Love can be expressed in two ways—verbal and nonverbal. Children are reassured when they see signs of affection between their parents. It builds confidence that there will be a home for them to visit after they are married and out on their own.

1. Read 2 Corinthians 12:14,15. What do you think of Paul's observation about parents and children?

____

____

____

____

Children should be the product of a healthy marriage, not the reason for its existence. Couples are wise to delay childbearing until they have had time to establish a solid marriage. It is unwise to have children as a means of solving problems in the marriage. It should never be assumed that children will cement a fragmented relationship.

2. What attitude is expressed in Psalm 127:3-5 towards having children? Explain why you agree or disagree with the Psalmist's perspective.

____

____

____

____

The empty nest period is a time to be anticipated and enjoyed. It offers couples tremendous opportunities. Among them are freedom of time, energy, and movement.

Freedom Of Time

Time previously devoted to planning for their children's care and welfare is now free for a couple to use for other plans. Parents who have wanted and enjoyed their children can look forward to when their children are mature. But this time must be anticipated and planned for if it is to be useful.

Freedom Of Energy

The empty nest releases energy which can be utilized for the welfare and happiness of the couple. Energy that was spent doing things for the children can now be diverted to things the parents have been waiting to do. Traveling, going back to school, entering a new or reentering an interrupted career are real options, especially for women who devoted themselves to staying home with the children.

Personality differences will dictate which direction this new freedom takes. With the lengthening life span and new opportunities open to maturing adults, there are many exciting things for empty nest parents to consider. This is especially true while they still feel young and vital in their middle years.

Freedom Of Movement

Never have adults had more opportunities for mobility. International travel and study beckon some; others park their recreational vehicles in exotic places they had only dreamed about. Some even unite this new-found freedom with Christian service. They join volunteer work crews building pioneer churches or work on the construction of Christian colleges at home or on the mission field.

ENRICHING MARRIAGE

Parents should begin early to help their children disengage from enmeshment in the family. They should take regular nights out, leaving the children with reliable caretakers. These should not always be relatives, for children need experience in being comfortable with a variety of caretakers.

Dinners out regularly and weekends away periodically without the children are good for both the parents and the children. This will prepare them for times when illness or tragedy require parents to be gone for an extended period of time. The children need to be prepared so they will not suffer separation anxiety or other psychological complications that result from enmeshment with their parents.

3. Read Genesis 2:24; Matthew 19:4-6; and Ephesians 5:31. Why do you think God repeated the same command in three different sections of the Bible—the Old Testament, the Gospels, and the Epistles?

____

____

____

____

How can you facilitate obedience to this command in your own family?

____

____

____

____

At birth, boys and girls are extremely similar, but by midlife they become as diverse as their gender and opportunities allow. Gail Sheehy has noted that by midlife, males and females are as different as they will ever be. Just as allowance for individual differences is made among children, so should it for their parents.

As couples grow older, however, they converge. By the end of life they are more similar than at any other point in their lives. When couples capitalize on their uniquenesses they can enjoy experiences in the workplace and in leisure-time activities. Midlife is a time for experimenting with new things—hobbies, recreation, games, flavors, fragrances, music, art, literature—and for exploring the cultural opportunities around them. Life takes on exciting dimensions for the midlife couple who explore their opportunities.

4. Read Proverbs 5:18,19. According to this passage, how does God feel about continued romantic love in a marriage?

____

____

____

____

Maintaining a vital romantic life throughout marriage is a challenge every couple must face. It is not always easy to be romantic in the midst of changing diapers, supervising homework, and teaching household chores. But, couples who work together in these living/learning experiences can maintain a level of communication that keeps their marriage above the humdrum of everyday life.

Keeping romance alive in marriage pays off as children develop interests outside the home and decide what to be when they grow up. Parents need to be working on the kind of marriage they want to have when they are free to enjoy the empty nest period of their lives. They have earned it!

Probably the most important activity a couple should perpetuate as they move through midlife is their devotions. This is the secret to maintaining an intimate relationship with God and a quality relationship with each other. Just because the children are gone is no reason to curtail family devotions. It is still family devotions, even if the family consists only of a mother and a father.

A significant part of maintaining a consistent devotional life is the attitude the couple have toward their finances. It is essential that they agree on how to handle money. Living within a reasonable budget, being consistent in paying tithes and giving offerings, and saving for retirement are part of Christian stewardship. Wrong attitudes toward the use of money can make it our master and rob us of intimacy with God.

5. Read Matthew 6:24. What is the spiritual result of not keeping one's attitude toward money in perspective?

____

____

____

____

____

6. What does James 4:7-10 tell us to do if we have determined that some aspect of our lives is out of spiritual focus?

EXPANDING YOUR IDENTITY

Midlife is the appropriate time to expand your personal identity to reach your God-given adult potential. This will include developing hobbies, recreation, and other pursuits. Many midlife adults were not given permission to play in their teens and early 20s because they had to assume responsibility for supporting themselves or helping their families survive. This is time to give oneself permission to play.

Midlife is a time to expand friendships. Friends come on different levels. Some are only acquaintances, others are known casually, but still others are close friends. Those on the highest level of friendship are confidants. While these relationships may be limited in number, they are essential.

Examine your "fan of friendships." Everyone needs at least five friends in each of five distinct areas of life: (1) the extended family; (2) the church family; (3) the world of work or career; (4) the world of hobbies and recreation; and (5) the community at large. The "fan of friendships" will become even more valuable as the children leave home and parents are faced with filling the time and space children used to occupy.

Midlife is also a wonderful time to take stock of the wisdom that has accrued with maturity and experience. We alluded to this in an earlier study as "sageing."

In the Old Testament, men of God such as Joshua and Samuel became known as seers (one who sees into the future) as they grew older. This does not refer to fortune-telling or psychic hot lines. These spiritual giants developed a special awareness about life that came with their intimate walk with God and they were highly esteemed in their time.

Time spent with God reflecting on His goodness can bring us to a place where younger people will seek us out for advice and guidance. "Sageing," then, becomes a form of Christian service.

7. Read Job 32:6-9. What was Elihu trying to convey to Job and his three older comforters?

8. **According to Psalm 90:12, how can we gain wisdom in the aging process?**

Hopefully, planning for retirement will have begun much earlier in life. This is the last stop before implementing the retirement plan. Couples need to examine their current resources and those they plan on accumulating before their actual retirement. Couples must make adequate plans before the customary retirement age of 65.

Many companies offer early retirement with a "golden handshake" (a bonus for early retirement) as part of their downsizing. Care needs to be taken in investing retirement monies and planning for additional income beyond social security, company pensions, and retirement bonuses. Frequently it is wise to seek professional advice in making these decisions.

9. **Read Proverbs 6:6-8. How can we profit by observing the ant?**

Under ordinary circumstances, one half of every couple will be a single survivor. Since we seldom know in advance which one it will be, it is important for a couple to discuss this potentiality. Every effort should be made for each to know all that will be necessary when he or she is left alone. This includes not only driving a car and handling the checkbook, but knowing the location of all valuables and being appraised of any obligations the couple may have incurred. This is no time for secrecy—it is a time for transparency so the survivor will not be overwhelmed after the funeral.

There is a direct correlation between how comfortable a person was as a single before marriage and how effective he or she will be as a surviving adult single. That is why it is important to explore the dimensions of singleness before marriage. Those skills have a way of returning upon demand after the death of a life's partner.

This is why neither one of the couple should lose his or her identity in the other. Each needs to develop a stable self-concept and be able to function adequately alone. Reluctance to discuss the will and funeral plans is a form of denial. Such vital information needs to be written and the location well-known to all members of the family.

Pitfalls To Avoid

Burnout

The word *burnout* was coined in 1974 by Herbert Freudenberg. It describes the progressive loss of idealism, energy, and purpose experienced by people who become overwhelmed by their work and the demands of life. Burnout refers to a depletion of energy, a dampened enthusiasm, and the loss of idealism. It comes to those who surrender to unrealistic demands of others and become disillusioned with life.

When life becomes routine rather than challenging, a person is a candidate for burnout. Enthusiasm dulls into stagnation; frustration sets in and leads to apathy. Dr. Archibald Hart offers five symptoms of burnout: (1) demoralization—a belief that you are no longer effective in your work; (2) depersonalization—treating yourself and others impersonally; (3) detachment—withdrawing from life's opportunities and responsibilities; (4) distancing—an avoidance of social and interpersonal contacts; and (5) defeatism—a feeling of being "beaten" and giving up hope.

The result is disengagement and the damage is primarily emotional. Exhaustion affects motivation and produces a loss of hope. As a result, there is a sense of helplessness and hopelessness which produces further discouragement. Creative interventions are needed to break the downward spiral and help you crawl out of the pit into which you have dug yourself. Burnout may never kill you, but life will not seem worth living until you regain a balanced perspective.

10. In Luke 10:38-42, what suggestions did Jesus give to Martha to help her avoid burnout?

____

____

____

____

How could you apply this principle to your life to prevent burnout?

____

____

____

____

Midlife Crisis

Jim Conway popularized the term "midlife crisis" in 1978 when he wrote *Men In Midlife Crisis*. He tells how he left his wife, children, and church. He found himself walking along a Gulf Coast beach. He said his experience was the result of depression which activated feelings of worthlessness, hopelessness, fatigue, and imaginary physical disorders. The victim of midlife crisis feels trapped and tied to a treadmill.

A few years later Jim's wife Sally wrote a companion book, *You And Your Husband's Midlife Crisis*, in which she revealed how she unwittingly contributed to her husband's midlife crisis. This, of course, was a form of codependency.

Symptoms of a midlife crisis are similar to those of burnout except there are more physical ramifications to the midlife crisis. In some ways it is related to what was referred to in a previous study as male menopause. Some people call it "the crazies." The unfortunate result of a midlife crisis is that it often results in leaving the family and introduces sexual acting out as part of working through the dilemma.

By midlife a man realizes he has reached the peak of his potential. If his aspirations and goals have not been met, his awareness of the shortness of time, with half of life already history, becomes foreboding. Conway says three forces converge to create the crisis: (1) the physical changes of midlife, (2) the psychological make-up that affects self-esteem, and (3) the social impact of being seen as aging. To this must be added a depletion of spiritual energy which results from lack of a constant and intimate walk with God.

A midlife crisis can happen more than once between the ages of 20 and 100. Most behavioral scientists are convinced that all men go through such a crisis to some degree. They assume it is as inevitable as adolescence following childhood. The truth is, however, that about a third of teenagers go through adolescence without turmoil. The same potential of escaping the snares of a turbulent midlife is open to those who maintain a vital relationship with God and their spouses through the passages of adulthood.

Burnout seems to be gender neutral—it is as common among women as men. A midlife crisis, however, is more of a masculine pitfall. Only those women who become competitive in the marketplace are susceptible to a midlife crisis. Even then it usually coincides with menopause.

11. Read Proverbs 3:7,8. How does Solomon suggest a man can avoid the ravages of a midlife crisis?

____

____

____

____

____

____

SUMMARY

In this study we have tried to discover ways of adjusting to life after the children have left home and to find happiness in the empty nest. We have noted that a fulfilling life-after-children awaits those who have kept their marital relationship vital and prepared adequately for these special years. Ways of enriching marriage during the developmental years of the children were discussed with the emphasis on keeping romance in marriage.

We have explored how couples can expand their identity and not lose it in their spouse. This is accomplished by expanding the fan of friendship and utilizing the wisdom that comes with years of experience. The importance of planning creatively for retirement was stressed with suggestions given for being content as a single survivor after the spouse has gone on to his/her eternal reward.

Finally, we explored how to avoid burnout and a midlife crisis, either of which could take all of the joy out of the later years and leave a legacy ranging from disappointment to despair.

Let's Review

1. What freedoms does the empty nest offer the midlife couple?

2. List four ways of enriching your marriage during midlife.

3. The fan of friendship should include what five kinds of individuals?

4. What is meant by sageing?

5. What are some of the ways a person can prepare to be a single survivor of a marriage?

6. Define either burnout or a midlife crisis, and list some creative interventions a person can make to avoid succumbing to one of these midlife pitfalls.

Study 9

Positive Aspects Of Aging

Aging has received a lot of bad press in recent years. But, as one octogenarian observed, "It is better than the alternative." A hundred years ago the average life span was so short (47 years) that aging was not considered a probability and seldom entered into family discussions. As the life span moved beyond the 70s into the 80s and now the 90s, those looking from the youthful end of the spectrum began to say, "You can't trust anyone over 30." Then they raised it to 40. Now those baby boomers are moving into the midlife they so freely decried.

In this study we want to examine the dimensions of aging and embrace the positive aspects of the process. Aging is to be anticipated, planned for, and accepted graciously, not dreaded. The Bible tells us the same God who made us also determines how long we will live on this earth. This life is only a prelude to eternal life with Him in heaven.

Intellectual Aspects Of Aging

In midlife we can take advantage of being at the peak of our potential. The expression used to be, "growing old gracefully." Maybe we should rephrase it to: "exploring today and anticipating tomorrow." Then we are free to focus on the goodness of the Lord in each decade of our life span.

The Bible extols three intellectual aspects of aging and shows they are each related to our awareness of the Lord.

Knowledge

Knowledge is the accumulation of information we gain through the lifespan. As we grow older, our memory banks expand to hold all of the facts, figures, and experiences we have tucked away for future reference.

Every time we have a meaningful thought there is a protein synthesis in the brain that records a residue of memory. All it takes to recall that memory is an adequate stimulus. It is the accumulation of knowledge in life that allows us to see God for who He is and develop a healthy attitude toward Him.

1. Read the story of the rich man and Lazarus (Luke 16:19-31). What evidence is there that the rich man had complete memory recall after his death?

____

____

____

Understanding

Understanding enables us to make sense out of the accumulated facts that compose our knowledge. If information is not meaningful, it is like nonsense syllables—it does us no good. In order to know God, we must understand who He is and what our relationship with Him was designed to be. Here is where we need the Holy Spirit to make known to us all of God's revelation so we can understand and obey Him (John 16:13).

Wisdom

Wisdom is more than the accumulation of knowledge. It is the application of that knowledge to the opportunities of life. Knowledge in itself is not sufficient to bring us into a right relationship with the Lord. We must understand what the Bible teaches and then apply it to the everyday activities of life. Our degree of wisdom is revealed by the way we interact with life and its challenges and opportunities.

2. Read Psalm 111:10 and Proverbs 1:7; 2:1-6; 9:10. Describe how knowledge, understanding, and wisdom interact in gaining a healthy fear (reverence) of the Lord.

____

____

____

Emotional Aspects Of Aging

Self-Esteem

A healthy self-esteem is essential for successful aging. Behavioral scientists have concluded that self-esteem (sometimes called the self-concept) is the single most significant factor in human behavior. Self-esteem is a judgment of personal worthiness that is expressed by the attitudes individuals hold towards themselves.

Self-esteem incorporates emotions, convictions, self-image, and self-talk. Whether a person's self-esteem is positive or faulty is reflected in his or her behavior.

Maurice Wagner suggests that there are three dimensions of self-esteem:

Belonging—having a sense of security and identity with others who love, accept, and support me. This involves an awareness of being wanted and accepted, of being cared for and enjoyed.

Worth—being affirmed as a person of value. This involves a sense of personal value, being cherished and respected, and leads to the feeling that "I am good" or "I am important."

Competence—being affirmed as an able person and gaining a sense of achievement from one's efforts. This involves feelings of adequacy, courage, helpfulness, and having strength enough to carry out the tasks of daily life.

On the other hand, faulty self-esteem paralyzes our potential, destroys our dreams, ruins our interpersonal relationships, and sabotages our work productiveness and Christian service. When individuals have faulty self-esteem, they need to correct their theology by reviewing the response of Jesus to the question, "What is the first commandment of all?" (Matthew 22:34-40; Luke 10:25-27).

People with a healthy self-concept know that their self-esteem comes from God, not from others. Cooperation with the leadership of the Holy Spirit is the secret to changing faulty self-esteem into a positive self-concept.

By midlife, most adults should have accumulated sufficient life experiences to support a healthy self-esteem which allows them to face the future with confidence. This includes the right to honor one's own uniqueness and to accept one's life as a gift from God. This permits individuals to build healthy relationships and to act toward others in nonthreatening ways. It also allows them to see and feel themselves as successful, to be self-confident, and to be assertive. This is seen in the ability to deal with fear and other strong emotions as well as the ability to share love with significant others.

3. How does Philippians 1:6 relate to a positive self-esteem?

____

____

____

4. Read Matthew 10:39-42. How do these words of Jesus impact our self-esteem?

____

____

____

Altruism

Altruism speaks of an unselfish concern for and devotion to the welfare of others. It is the opposite of egoism. Those who have a positive self-esteem will be more interested in promoting the welfare of others than in having their own way.

Altruism is illustrated in the actions of the Good Samaritan who provided for the welfare of a stranger who had fallen on hard times on the Jericho Road (Luke 10:30-37).

5. How does the commandment stated in Mark 12:31 relate to altruism?

____

____

____

____

VOCATIONAL ASPECTS OF AGING

By midlife, an adult has had the opportunity of collecting a half century of experiences. How they use the opportunities of life will be determined by whether they view aging positively or negatively.

A schoolteacher retired after 40 years in the classroom. When someone said, "She has had 40 years of experience," her superintendent remarked, "No, she has not had 40 years of experience, she has had 1 year of experience 40 times."

There is a difference in facing each new challenge as an opportunity and in repeating the same set of responses year after year. The midlife adult who has profited from each eventuality in life will accumulate a wealth of experience. This experience becomes the basis of new experiences yet to come as he or she explores the positive aspects of aging.

6. Read Genesis 2:15. Why was Adam placed in the Garden of Eden?

____

____

____

____

____

Was the assignment given Adam a result of the Fall? (Genesis 3:19). Or, was it given before the Fall? Your answer will identify whether you see work as a privilege or a punishment. Which is it?

One of the things that makes work meaningful is a sense of creativity. Research has proven that monotonous work is much more stressful than work in which people can express their creativity. The attitude one has toward work determines whether it is perceived as creative or mundane.

7. Read Ecclesiastes 2:4-11,18,20. After he had accumulated his wealth and accomplished tremendous feats of work, what was the writer's conclusion?

8. After reading Ecclesiastes 2:23, detail below why the writer of Ecclesiastes grieved as he looked back over his accomplishments.

9. Read Ecclesiastes 2:24 and 5:19. How do you account for the writer's sudden change in attitude?

10. Compare Ecclesiastes 9:10 with Colossians 3:23,24. What attitude does the writer of Ecclesiastes display regarding a work ethic in comparison with Paul's?

The peak vocational experience is conquest—to be able to learn a task and conquer it. This is more than a casual approach to the world of work. It is giving each task your very best and carrying it out in such a way that you become a master craftsman.

Commit the first part of Ecclesiastes 9:10 to memory. It will encourage you to anticipate the work opportunities that will come your way in the future. The past is prelude; the future is filled with challenges. This will be especially true when you reach the retirement phase of life.

LOVING ASPECTS OF AGING

Dr. and Mrs. Frank Minirth, Dr. and Mrs. Brian Newman, and Dr. and Mrs. Robert Hemfelt of the Minirth-Meier clinics have examined how love develops through the years in marriage partners who are committed to each other. They have written *Passages Of Marriage* to share their findings. They observe the following passages.

Spontaneous Love

The first 2 years of marriage are marked by spontaneous love. This is when two extremely different and independent persons weld into one marital unit. This follows "leaving and cleaving" and is what God calls a "one flesh" union.

11. Read Genesis 2:24 and list the steps newlyweds pass through in developing a spontaneous love.

Realistic Love

The 3rd to the 10th years of marriage are a time of developing a realistic view of the relationship. All of the "happily ever after" fantasies are exposed to the reality of two very different people, one male and the other female, finding balance and equality in their relationship. It is during this time that many couples discover that "love is a many splendored thing."

Failure to be honest about a couple's differences, however, or about their shared goals, can direct the marriage away from the mainstream of life and toward the shoals of conflict.

12. How can transparency be affirmed and maintained in a maturing marriage according to Genesis 2:25?

How can this be accomplished in areas that transcend the physical?

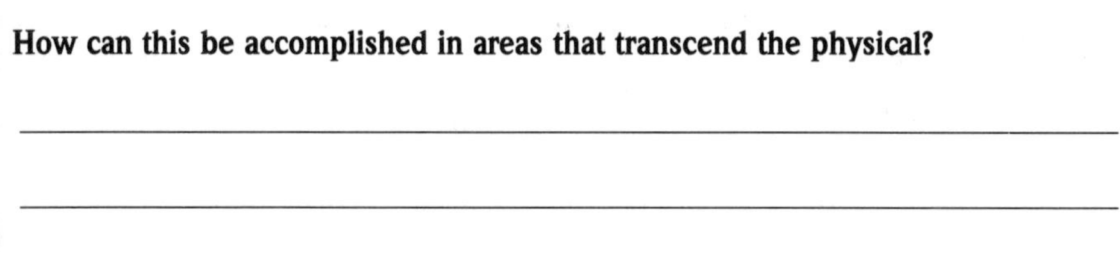

Comfortable Love

Years 11 to 25 invite the couple to settle into a comfortable love. During these years the couple must learn how to maintain an individual identity along with a marriage identity.

In this era, a couple will need to explore the dimensions of forgiveness and learn to accept the inevitable lessons that aging and the passing of time bring into the marriage. A major task in this stage is guiding the children from childhood into adolescence and preparing them to enter adulthood as fully functioning individuals.

Balancing dreams with realities is a challenge to a couple. They must face squarely the goals they will never attain and the dreams that will not materialize. If a couple has developed intimacy with each other and with God, these can be comfortable years. Unfortunately, couples who have not worked on their relationship effectively threaten divorce about this time in the marriage, which coincides with the youngest child leaving home.

Renewing Love

The decade between the 26th and 35th year of marriage is an appropriate time to concentrate on the renewal of love in the relationship. Hopefully, the children will be on their own, and the couple can focus on each other without the distraction maturing children can bring.

By this time the couple should have accepted that neither one of them is perfect. To become comfortable with the imperfect, without attempts to change the other, is a major step toward renewing love in the marriage. The "blame game" should have been left behind and the energy of conflict directed toward consolidating the stability of the marriage.

Transcendent Love

The continuing challenge after the 35th year of marriage is to develop a transcendent love. The couple rises above the mundane in life and focuses on making the retirement years all they have the potential to be. "Transcendent love is a profound and peaceful perspective toward your partner and toward life," the Minirths, Newmans, and Hemfelts concluded. This is the time to accept the one and only life God has extended to each of His creation.

As transcendent love grows, the perspective of life shifts from "death is an end" to "death is a beginning" and from "death invalidates life" to "death completes life."

SPIRITUAL ASPECTS OF AGING

Intimacy With God

Intimacy with God can grow only as an individual seeks time to be alone with God. It is illustrated in the words of an old song: "Shut in with God in the secret place, there in the Spirit beholding His face."

As the years go by and the couple is back to just a twosome, it is important to maintain a personal devotional life. This will include Bible reading, prayer, praise, and meditation. When this is buttressed with couple devotions, a shared time with each other and with God, the intimacy of the marriage grows both horizontally and vertically. This embellishes a marriage that is becoming transcendent and provides a spiritual dimension in marriage that the secular society cannot comprehend.

13. Read Philippians 3:10,11. What can a couple learn from Paul's prayer for intimacy with God?

____

____

____

Contentment With Life

Contentment is a legitimate goal in life (1 Timothy 6:6). But, it needs to be accompanied by godliness. As the years pass by, the couple can expect to experience more contentment in their personal lives as well as their marital life.

Contentment, however, does not imply complacency. When contentment develops in our relationship with God, it will keep us actively concerned with the things that concern Him. Whereas complacency is passive and withdraws people from involvement with life, contentment is active and keeps us alert to become all God wants us to become. This kind of contentment was experienced by the apostle Paul and shared in his letter to the first church he founded in Europe.

14. Read Philippians 4:11-13. List the three dimensions of contentment Paul had discovered as he was strengthened by the Lord in his walk with Him.

____

____

____

SUMMARY

In this study we have looked at the intellectual aspects of aging and noted the interaction between knowledge, understanding, and wisdom. Then we looked at the relationship between self-esteem and altruism as part of the emotional aspects of aging. Vocationally, we contrasted experience, creativity, and conquest.

Bringing together these aspects of aging make it possible for the couple to explore how love matures: spontaneous love grows into realistic love which leads to comfortable love that matures into renewing love that has the potential to become transcendent. This developmental sequence is available to every Christian couple.

Finally we looked at intimacy with God and contentment with life as they interact in exploring the spiritual aspects of aging. Couples who develop in these aspects of aging are guaranteed a love life that is both rewarding and fulfilling.

LET'S REVIEW

1. List the three intellectual views of aging that Solomon says are foundational for a reverent walk with God.

2. Contrast the difference between healthy and faulty self-esteem.

3. List three vocational aspects of aging that are vital to the self-esteem of a worker.

4. List the five stages in developing a mature love in marriage.

5. In which of the above listed stages are you in your own marriage? What challenges must you face in order to move on to the next stage of love?

6. How can contentment in life lead to greater intimacy with God?

MOVING ON

God has been actively involved in our lives from our beginnings. He continues to sustain us as we progress through the transitions of aging until our final phase of aging which telescopes into eternal life through the transition commonly known as death.

We experience a series of changes in a lifetime. The first phase is represented by growth and development in all aspects of life: physical, intellectual, emotional, spiritual, and social. Then we reach a plateau in adolescence and slowly begin the descent into adulthood and its passages of aging. All the time we are moving on.

We recognize that our earlier years were designed to prepare us to face the older adult years of life. Reflecting over a life span causes celebration when we realize we have been led by the Lord and have faced the challenges of life through His power and strength. In the process, we discover that we are no longer fearful of moving on.

Psychosocial Challenges Of Older Adulthood

The final stage of life, older adulthood, is rooted in how well we have traversed the previous passages of young and middle adulthood. This is when we weave the threads of life into a final pattern that reveals a life well-lived or one that was dissipated. Eric Erikson says the challenge of this final stage is to experience success through integrity. Otherwise, despair will spoil the final pattern of a life that will be viewed by our posterity long after we are gone.

Erikson suggests that the man or woman who is to achieve integrity is the one who handles the challenges of previous eras adequately. He or she will move into the older adult years with a sense of ego identity that is wholesome. This person will be able to face the later years with the resolve that comes from accepting adjustments to change.

From infancy on we strive for maturity—achieving full adult form, structure, and function. In the older years we look back over the life span and appreciate the continuity of life that brings us to the next level of discovery.

Abraham Maslow's description of the "self-actualized" person suggests that the mature person is oriented to the real world, not a bundle of fantasies. He or she accepts who they and others actually are. This demonstrates a high degree of spontaneity. This person is problem-centered rather than self-centered, as well as autonomous and independent with a fresh appreciation for life.

The mature person maintains deep and intimate relationships with a small circle of carefully selected friends. He or she is democratic in value orientation and understands the difference between means to achieve a goal and the rightful ends to be achieved. This person exhibits a good sense of humor, is creative and open to new experiences, and resists sarcasm and cruelty.

As a Christian, the mature person adjusts to the challenges of life as measured by his or her concept of the kingdom of heaven and the will of God. This process may be called "Christ-actualization" and is the embodiment of Galatians 2:20—total identification with Christ.

1. Read Psalm 23:6. How did David express his belief that God's presence would transcend life and death?

____

____

____

____

Integrity represents a love for humankind that is distinct from the narcissistic self-love of childhood. It is the culmination of the quest for order and meaning and the acceptance of an individual's life cycle as absolute. It means realizing a new and different love for one's parents, free of the desire that they should have been different or given more opportunities to their offspring.

Integrity represents an acceptance of the fact that one's life is one's own responsibility and blame or shame cannot be placed on significant others. It involves a comradeship with men and women of history who created order and objects and sayings conveying their concept of human dignity and love.

Although aware of the relativity of all the various lifestyles which give meaning to human striving, the one who possesses integrity is ready to defend his or her own lifestyle against all physical and economic threats. This person knows that an individual life is the impact of one life cycle with one segment of history, and that for him or her, all human integrity rests with the one style of integrity in which he or she has participated.

2. Read Psalm 119:153-160. How did David demonstrate his acceptance of his life cycle and lifestyle?

____

____

____

3. After reading 1 Timothy 6:6-9, note below how Paul expressed his contentment with God's will for his life.

____

____

____

____

Fortunately, integrity in the older adult years allows for flexibility and role changes. It allows for all of the adjustments we will discuss in the developmental tasks of aging later in this study. This resilience comes from attitudes and skills learned in the earlier stages of life.

4. Read Ecclesiastes 7:2. How would this perspective help an individual make plans for his or her future?

____

____

____

____

5. Read 2 Timothy 1:12. How might adopting an attitude such as Paul's help an individual face the inevitabilities of life?

____

____

____

____

This is the ultimate test of integrity—to face death without fear or apprehension and to move beyond bargaining to acceptance of death and life after death.

6. Compare Romans 8:35-39 and Philippians 1:21. How did Paul express his faith in God's ultimate victory in life and in death?

Failure to achieve integrity in the final segment of life leads to despair.

Despair is expressed by feelings that time is too short to attempt to start over again and experiment with alternate roads to fulfillment.

7. How did Sarah respond to God's promise to give her a child in her post-childbearing years? (Genesis 18:10-12).

---

8. Read Genesis 21:1,2,5. When did God answer His promise of a son to Abraham and Sarah?

Despair is revealed when meaning is not found in life, for the unexamined life is a life without meaning. *Man's Search For Meaning*, which describes Viktor Frankl's experiences in a Nazi prison camp during the Holocaust, tells how he survived inhumane indignities. He said to his captors: "You may strip me of my clothes and all my possessions, but you cannot rob me of my dignity." Frankl maintained his faith in God and his integrity, challenging a whole generation with his writings.

9. After reading Psalm 14:1, detail below God's opinion of those who deny His existence and intervention in the affairs of mankind.

---

10. Read Ecclesiastes 1:2-11. Summarize the writer's opinion of human existence. How might this attitude affect the way a person lived his or her own life?

The person in despair shows disgust or a chronic contemptuous displeasure with particular institutions and/or people. Such displeasure only signifies the individual's contempt for himself or herself.

11. Read Matthew 25:24-30. How did the faithless servant show his contempt for himself and his master?

The futility of a second chance is ignored as the person in despair bargains for more time with more advantages in an extended life. Those who face death without hope in Christ are prone to this futile attempt to avoid the inevitable (Hebrews 9:27).

12. Read Luke 16:19-26. How did the rich man bargain for a second chance at life?

Regret over lost opportunities, compounded by a fear of death, plague the aging person who has not explored the upper dimensions of life's potentials. It shows on his or her face. It is revealed in attitudes. And, unfortunately, it leads to loneliness which compounds despair in the face of death.

13. Read Psalms 71:9 and 102:23. What emotion regarding death is the Psalmist communicating through these psalms?

14. Read Matthew 13:49,50. Why do unbelievers have a right to fear death?

DEVELOPMENTAL TASKS OF AGING

Physical strength continues to decrease in older adulthood, especially in men. The incidence of heart attacks increases and it takes longer for the body to recover from strenuous exercise. The taste buds become less sensitive and the efficiency of smell decreases with age as does visual acuity, leading to presbyopia (old sight) or far-sightedness. Brighter illumination is required for reading and glasses may have to be changed more frequently.

The upper range of sound continues to decrease and again this is more pronounced in men than women. Breathing becomes more difficult with the decline in basal metabolic rate. Abraham Lincoln, the great Emancipator of U.S. history who freed the slaves in the 19th century, observed, "After 40, a man is responsible for his own face."

15. What was Eli's physical condition at the time of his death at age 98 as recorded in 1 Samuel 4:14,15?

16. Read 1 Kings 1:1-4. What was David's physical condition? How did the servants attempt to minister to him? What was the result?

Retirement frequently coincides with the transition from midlife into older adulthood. It is too late now to initiate retirement plans but the inevitability of adjusting to a reduced income looms on the horizon.

Any financial preplanning the couple have done to insure the security of their golden years will be invaluable at this point in life. Hopefully, the home and car will be paid for and the family debt eradicated. Budgeting within the limitations of a fixed income becomes as much a challenge as it was when the couple first married years ago.

17. According to Matthew 6:33,34, what is the proper perspective of material things in one's life?

It is important to maintain meaningful friendships within one's age group. People born within the same chronological period are frequently called a "cohort group." They have more in common than those born a generation before or a generation after them. This is important while both of the couple are living, but even more essential when one of them has gone on to his or her eternal reward.

In the declining years, with the accompanying decrease in physical vitality, it is important to be located in satisfactory housing. It is wise for the couple to maintain the family home as long as possible, but there comes a time when they will need to move to smaller accommodations with more supervision.

It is not always wise to move in with adult children. Careful consideration needs to be given to the extra strains that will be put on three generations living under one roof. Moving to a retirement center or apartment before going into nursing facilities allows for a less traumatic transition from the family home to the nursing home.

Losing a spouse is one of the most difficult transitions of life. This is true at any age, but especially when the couple are in their golden years and have been inseparable since retirement. That is why it is important that the couple's wills be brought up to date periodically and funeral plans and arrangements for burial made. These decisions are too important to be left to a time when emotions are high and grief grips and chills the heart.

18. Read Genesis 23:1,2 and show how Abraham responded to the death of Sarah.

19. How did Jacob respond to the premature death of Rachel in childbirth? (Genesis 35:18-20).

Maintaining an intimate, personal relationship with God is important at any age, but especially as one is approaching the end of this life and the transition into eternal life. Continuing to attend church is important as long as a person has the strength to go. Even when you are no longer driving, it is appropriate to arrange for transportation to and from services.

Daily devotions are essential and should not stop when one is left alone. Reading the Bible is enhanced by using a large-print Bible. A magnifying glass may be necessary for reading other kinds of Christian literature. Listening to the Bible on tape as well as books and sermons on tape can keep a devotional atmosphere in the home at all times. And, Christian music on tape is conducive to both meditation and praise.

20. Read Revelation 1:9-20. What evidence does the believer have that Christ has ultimate power over hell and death?

____

____

____

____

____

____

____

____

____

____

SUMMARY

In this study we have looked at the psychosocial changes individuals face in older adulthood. Success in this process is revealed in a person's integrity. This includes an appreciation for the continuity of life, an acceptance of one's life cycle and lifestyle, cooperation with the inevitabilities of life, and an acceptance of death.

Failure to meet the challenges of this period leads to complaining that time is too short, failure to find meaning in human existence, loss of faith in self and others, and wanting a second chance at life. The ultimate despair is the fear of death which haunts those who have not prepared appropriately for life after death.

We next looked at the developmental tasks every aging person faces. The quality of the golden years is established by how well one anticipates and carries out these necessary tasks: (1) adjusting to decreasing physical strength, (2) adjusting to retirement and reduced income, (3) establishing an explicit affiliation with one's age group, (4) establishing satisfactory living arrangements, (5) adjusting to the death of a spouse, and (6) crystallizing an intimate, personal relationship with God.

LET'S REVIEW

1. How does an elderly person demonstrate he or she has successfully met the challenges of old age with integrity?

2. What are the evidences of despair as one faces the end of life?

3. What are the developmental tasks an elderly person faces during the final stages of aging?

4. Read Ecclesiastes 12:1-7. Enumerate the descriptions of the physical aging process that are hidden in this passage.

5. Looking back over this series of studies, what have you learned that will help you face your own aging with confidence and assurance?